CHAUCER AND BECKET'S MOTHER:
THE MAN OF LAW'S TALE, CONVERSION,
AND RACE IN THE MIDDLE AGES

MEDIEVAL MEDIA AND CULTURE

Further Information and Publications
www.arc-humanities.org/our-series/arc/mmc/

CHAUCER AND BECKET'S MOTHER:
THE MAN OF LAW'S TALE, CONVERSION, AND RACE IN THE MIDDLE AGES

by
MERIEM PAGÈS

First and foremost, this book is dedicated to the boys:
Robert, Nick, George, and Robbie.
But it is also for the women:
Those who sought distant, foreign shores to dream their dreams of happiness and love—Erminie Pagès and Odette Pispicot, Valérie Lebreil and Valérie Pagès.
Those who stayed home and dared to challenge others' perceptions of them, especially Nicole Pagès.
My niece, Hannah Ellen Peterlin, the bravest modern Saracen princess I know.
My nieces, Florence Marguerite and Sophie Marguerite, who have already pursued their dreams across several continents.
My granddaughters, Madelyn Sullivan MacDonald and Olivia Grace MacDonald, who have yet to find their place in our crazy, ever-changing world.
And, of course, this book is also dedicated to Becket's mommy, sipping her Appletini and scowling at me while she calls her Uber...

British Library Cataloguing in Publication Data

A catalogue record for this book is available from the British Library.

© 2023, Arc Humanities Press, Leeds

The authors assert their moral right to be identified as the authors of their part of this work.

Permission to use brief excerpts from this work in scholarly and educational works is hereby granted provided that the source is acknowledged. Any use of material in this work that is an exception or limitation covered by Article 5 of the European Union's Copyright Directive (2001/29/EC) or would be determined to be "fair use" under Section 107 of the U.S. Copyright Act September 2010 Page 2 or that satisfies the conditions specified in Section 108 of the U.S. Copyright Act (17 USC §108, as revised by P.L. 94-553) does not require the Publisher's permission.

ISBN (HB): 9781641894500
eISBN (PDF): 9781802701043

www.arc-humanities.org

Printed and bound in the UK (by CPI Group [UK] Ltd), USA (by Bookmasters), and elsewhere using print-on-demand technology.

CONTENTS

List of Illustrations vii

Acknowledgements ix

Introduction. Desire, Anxiety, and Conversion 1

Chapter 1. Anxieties of Conversion in High and Late Medieval Literature. 13

Chapter 2. Thomas Becket's Mother. 35

Chapter 3. The Becket Legend, *The Man of Law's Tale*, and Conversion. 61

Chapter 4. *The Man of Law's Tale* in Context 77

Conclusion. 91

Bibliography 99

Index 105

LIST OF ILLUSTRATIONS

Figure 1. Bas-de-page scene of the mother of Thomas, the Saracen Emir's daughter, being recognized by Gilbert Becket's servant. 54

Figure 2. Detail of a bas-de-page of the mother of Thomas of Canterbury being baptized, immersed in a large font, by two bishops 54

Figure 3. Bas-de-page scene of the mother of Thomas Becket, the Saracen Emir's daughter, being married to Gilbert Becket. 55

Figure 4. Bas-de-page scene of Thomas Becket's mother lying in bed with the infant Thomas beside her in a cradle and a woman holding back the curtain... 55

Table 1. Information about Thomas Becket's mother in historical accounts that provide some details about his parents............................ 37

ACKNOWLEDGEMENTS

I owe a huge debt of gratitude to many for helping me complete this manuscript. I will begin by thanking everyone who kindly let me drone on endlessly for months and years, especially Robert G. Sullivan, Anna Louise Joseph, Laura Pontani, Celia Rabinowitz, Marie Duggan, and Margaret Orelup.

Then there are those who helped me research specific lines of inquiry: Meredith Clermont-Ferrand who guided me through important literature about the Lollards and their articles of faith and Jenna Hall, my brilliant research assistant, who conducted research on colour-blind casting in contemporary "medieval" films. Although I did not pursue either of these lines of inquiry in the end, I am deeply grateful to Meredith and Jenna and plan on returning to both subjects in future teaching and research projects. There are also those who read and re-read several versions of the manuscript: Robin Dizard who read an early draft, the amazing Angela Jane Weisl who read too many drafts to remember and yet still asked to see the final version, the incomparable Robert G. Sullivan, and Anna Henderson, editor extraordinaire at Arc Humanities Press. A huge thank you must also go out to Lena Brown, who helped me sort myself out when I had written myself into a corner and otherwise kept me going by allowing me to visualize Alis and Connie exchanging their (very different) views of the world in grungy LA bars...

Thanks are also due to Keene State College for all of the emotional and financial support I received throughout the writing process. I am thankful to Jamie Landau and Faculty Enrichment for the Faculty Enrichment grant that allowed me to start working in earnest on the project in the summer of 2018. I am also profoundly grateful to Dean Celia Rabinowitz for her support and patience as I bumbled my way through two Faculty Development Grant applications. Finally, I would certainly not have completed this project without receiving a sabbatical leave in the fall of 2020. Although taking my sabbatical in that particular semester meant that I did not get to write until the evening when little people were asleep, the opportunity to focus on research rather than teaching proved essential to revising and finishing this study.

Also crucial to completing this project were two very specific initiatives at Keene State College: The Daily Writing Habit group, led by Amber Davisson, and biannual faculty writing retreats organized and planned by Katherine Tirabassi. I began writing the very first draft of my introduction shortly after Amber held our first weekly meeting, I finished the first draft of the second chapter in May 2018 at the end of that year's Writing Retreat, and I finished drafting the third and fourth chapters in January 2019 at our midwinter retreat. The final revisions to my manuscript were made at the retreat of May 2022. My experience with this project shows the tremendous impact faculty and institutional support can have on research, particularly for female faculty with young children.

Speaking of young children, the time has come for me to thank two very special people: George Hassan Jacques Pagès-Sullivan and Robert Bernard Rashid Pagès-Sullivan. In many ways, this project has framed their lives. I began it around the time George first started to point with his finger and being able to let me know where he wanted to go after school, and my sabbatical was divided between thinking about ways to help George navigate special education and speech therapy remotely during the day and untangling my research on Becket's mother and *The Man of Law's Tale* at night. Robbie and this project are also singularly connected. I finished the first draft of an early version of my manuscript while in the early process of labour, read Geraldine Heng's book with Robbie sprawled over me during naptime shortly after the onset of COVID, and revised and resubmitted at the end of his first year of daycare. George and Robbie, the two of you make everything better. Always.

And last, but certainly not least, I must return to Robert G. Sullivan, my wonderful, amazing, rock-star husband who, in addition to being the best dad a boy could have—TRACTOR!—also continuously helped me work on this project, giving me book after book to help me with my research, always asking me about how the project was going, and continuously engaging with me and arguing with me to ensure that my argument was as sharp and conclusive as possible. While any mistakes in the following study are undoubtedly mine, anything good no less doubtfully belongs to Robert. Thank you, Robert, for your incredible support and endless generosity. This book would never have been written were it not for you!

Introduction

DESIRE, ANXIETY, AND CONVERSION

A man from a historically oppressed minority community is accused of a crime committed not far from where he lives. Although there is a dearth, if any, evidence for his having perpetrated this crime, he is arrested, tried, and sentenced to death.

This short paragraph provides a loose description of what happened to Julius Jones, a forty-one-year-old man imprisoned for over twenty years for a crime he claims he did not commit—and for which the evidence has proven ambiguous at best. After a widespread national campaign and heavy mediatization about the case, Jones's execution was cancelled by Oklahoma Governor Stitt only four hours prior to the time for which it was scheduled on November 18, 2021.[1] Many other death row inmates—also black men, also incarcerated for most of their lives, also convicted without careful weighing of the evidence against them, and sometimes suffering from diagnosed learning and cognitive disabilities—were not so fortunate and died at the hands of their state.

But the paragraph above describes not only the experience of Julius Jones and other Black men in the contemporary United States, but also that of Mandl, one of countless German men arrested and sentenced to death in late fifteenth-century Passau, Germany because of his Jewish faith. In Mandl's case, his execution was not stayed at the eleventh hour, and his conversion only served to save him from the fire. As a newly Christian man, he was beheaded rather than burnt alive.[2]

Race in/and the Middle Ages

In opening this introductory chapter in this manner, I hope to emphasize the similarities between these two episodes, ones so far removed in time and space, culture and environment, yet also rendered similar by the harassment and oppression of marginalized individuals. In both cases, men from minority communities are identified, apprehended, and murdered by the very legal system which should provide some respite from continuous harassment.

It is these similarities and the questions they raise about the origins of racism in medieval Western Europe that lie at the heart of the debate about race in the Middle Ages. This debate and the many scholarly articles and monographs devoted to it, as captured by Jonathan Hsy and Julie Orlemanski in their bibliography, "Race and Medieval Studies: A Partial Bibliography," has gone on for at least thirty years.[3] At the root of the

---

1 "Gov. Stitt Grants Julius Jones Clemency—8 Facts You Need to Know About his Case," Innocence Project, https://innocenceproject.org/julius-jones-death-row-oklahoma-what-to-know/.

2 Miri Rubin, *Gentile Tales: The Narrative Assault on Late Medieval Jews* (New Haven: Yale University Press, 1999), 87.

3 Jonathan Hsy and Julie Orlemanski, "Race and Medieval Studies: A Partial Bibliography," *postmedieval*, 8, no. 4 (2017): 500–31.

debate about race and medieval Europe is the question of when race emerges as a concept. Traditionally, race is seen as a modern construct born in Renaissance Spain at the moment in the fifteenth century when individuals who converted from Islam and Judaism to Christianity came to be barred from official positions in spite of their conversion.[4] David Nirenberg pertinently draws together various attitudes towards a range of minorities in medieval Europe in his 1996 *Communities of Violence: Persecution of Minorities in the Middle Ages*:

> There are different opinions, of course, as to when a "tolerant" European Middle Ages turned bad. Historians of Jews, Muslims, heretics, gay people, and lepers have all placed the shift at different dates, ranging from the First Crusade...forward. Most recently Carlo Ginzburg has argued for a later date, claiming that there emerged in the first half of the fourteenth century...an irrational fear of conspiracy which had previously been repressed in the European mentality: a belief that certain groups, whether Jews, lepers, or witches, were conspiring to destroy society.[5]

Nirenberg's turning point has typically been associated with the replacement of the "religious divides" of the medieval era by a "theory of races, which defined a ... division of humankind into subspecies placed in a hierarchy."[6] In his seminal essay on the subject, "Medieval and Modern Concepts of Race and Ethnicity," Robert Bartlett strongly argues for the use of the term "ethnicity" rather than "race" in referring to medieval community identity and formation.[7] Conversely, others, including Jeffrey Jerome Cohen, Dorothy Kim, James M. Thomas, and Cord J. Whitaker, have argued just as forcibly for the use of "race" in reference to medieval European history and literature.[8] James M. Thomas succinctly describes this position on the topic:

---

[4] Benzion Netanyahu, *The Origins of the Inquisition in Fifteenth Century Spain* (New York: Random House, 1995), 983, as quoted in James M. Thomas, "The Racial Formation of Medieval Jews: A Challenge to the Field," *Ethnic and Racial Studies*, 30, no. 10 (2010): 1749. In *The Origins of Racism in the West*, Charles de Miramon notes that the term "race" is first used to refer to hunting dogs in France, "not Spain or Portugal" while Valentin Groebner argues that anxiety over sexual mixing and miscegenation existed in Spain but not in Italy and other parts of Europe in the fourteenth and fifteenth centuries. Charles de Miramon, "Noble Dogs, Noble Blood: The Invention of the Concept of Race in the Late Middle Ages," in *The Origins of Racism in the West*, ed. Miriam Eliav-Feldon, Benjamin Isaac, and Joseph Ziegler (Cambridge: Cambridge University Press, 2009), 201 and Valentin Groebner, "The Carnal Knowing of a Coloured Body: Sleeping with Arabs and Blacks in the European Imagination, 1300–1550," in Eliav-Feldon, Isaac, and Ziegler, *The Origins of Racism in the West*, 225–26.

[5] David Nirenberg, *Communities of Violence: Persecution of Minorities in the Middle Ages* (Philadelphia: University of Pennsylvania Press, 1996), 4.

[6] Francisco Bethencourt, *Racisms: From the Crusades to the Twentieth Century* (Princeton: Princeton University Press, 2014), 3.

[7] Robert Bartlett, "Medieval and Modern Concepts of Race and Ethnicity," *Journal of Medieval and Early Modern Studies*, 31, no. 1 (Winter 2001): 39–56.

[8] Jeffrey Jerome Cohen, "Race," in *A Handbook of Middle English Studies*, ed. Marion Turner (Chichester: Wiley, 2013), 109–22; Dorothy Kim, "Reframing Race and Jewish/Christian Relations in the Middle Ages," *transversal*, 13, no. 1 (2015): 56; Thomas, "The Racial Formation of Medieval Jews," 1737–55; and Cord J. Whitaker, *Black Metaphors: How Modern Racism Emerged from Medieval Race-Thinking* (Philadelphia: University of Pennsylvania Press, 2019).

While the vocabularies of difference may have altered in their rhetorical form from early medieval descriptions of impurity which could be cured through conversion, to late medieval depictions of essential and corporeal inferiority, to the scientific descriptions of biological impurity—the images of the Jew as black, as threatening, and as a demon to both the Christian spirit and the newly formed nation-state persisted over time (see Gilman 1991). The language of nineteenth-century medical science only transmuted earlier assumptions of innate difference from that of the soul to that of the body, but the sociopolitical consequences were quite similar.[9]

An especially important contributor to this conversation is Geraldine Heng, who has spent much of her career ensuring that medieval European race-making be more visible to medievalists and non-medievalists alike. In her groundbreaking study, *Empire of Magic: Medieval Romance and the Politics of Cultural Fantasy*, Heng recasts medieval romance as a nation-building tool, a genre conceived in the trauma of the First Crusade.[10] Here, Heng examines the ways in which romance both supports dominant power structures and hierarchies—for example, by privileging the knightly class over archers—while establishing a proto-nationalistic English identity through setting up various Others as negative foils.[11] It is in describing this process that Heng first articulates the concept of "race-religion," a term that redefines race as determined not only through biology but also through culture and religion.[12]

Heng further elaborates on the concept of "race-religion" and the medieval roots of racism in *The Invention of Race in the European Middle Ages*, providing a detailed analysis of the racialization of Jews in England in the twelfth and thirteenth centuries before turning to the treatment of other groups—Africans, Muslims, Mongols, Native Americans, and Romani—in late medieval Europe.[13] Throughout her significant body of work, Heng disrupts medievalists' tendency to repress uncomfortable passages in medieval works and relegate the origins of race to the Early Modern period.

Heng's adoption of the term "race" to discuss medieval European prejudices against marginalized communities is instrumental to achieving this end. Early on in *The Invention of Race*, Heng argues that such terminology provides access to tools otherwise not available to medieval scholars.[14] Using the vocabulary of modern racial discourse renders the issues and texts under discussion much more pressing and calls our attention to medieval European intolerance in a way that other terms, more conventionally used to study the representation of the Other in medieval Europe, do not. Words such as "anti-Judaism" and "anti-Muslim" safely distance us from the Middle Ages; by contrast "race" is loaded with meaning that resonates intimately with modern readers.

---

9 Thomas, "The Racial Formation of Medieval Jews," 1751.

10 Geraldine Heng, *Empire of Magic: Medieval Romance and the Politics of Cultural Fantasy* (New York: Columbia University Press, 2003).

11 Heng, *Empire of Magic*, 128–46.

12 Heng first defines this term in her discussion of the Constance story. Heng, *Empire of Magic*, 234.

13 Geraldine Heng, *The Invention of Race in the European Middle Ages* (Cambridge: Cambridge University Press, 2018).

14 Heng, *Invention of Race*, 4.

If Heng argues for the use of the term "race" in the medieval European context to highlight the processes by which difference is marked in the Middle Ages, Cord J. Whitaker points out the significance of discussing race in premodern Western Europe for our own contemporary world. Whitaker concludes his *Black Metaphors* by highlighting that the debate about race in medieval Europe is not simply an academic dispute about something in the past but, rather, a question that continues to influence the way we see and perceive one another today:

> Arguments that race is not germane to the Middle Ages, that it does not apply and should not be discussed, amount to the acceptance of the rhetorical mirage of medieval whiteness. While the Middle Ages in the Western, European and American contexts, are often taken as a symbol representing white people—what is most studied in Western universities is medieval Europe rather than developments in Africa or Asia during the same period—rhetorical mirage dictates that the distance between signified and sign collapses until whiteness appears to signify the medieval past. Until whiteness *is* the Middle Ages.[15]

How we feel about race and medieval Europe has and will continue to have a powerful impact on us in the here and now.

In addition to the question of whether the Middle Ages itself or the present day should be the focal point in the discussion about race and the Middle Ages, there exist other facets to the issue. Not only is it the case that, as Maghan Keita—amongst many others—has argued, we need "to unpack—to disengage—our current racial attitudes from the medieval Europe they have constructed," but there is also a need to address wider cultural differences between medieval Europe and modern society if we are serious about trying to understand medieval approaches to non-dominant groups and communities in Western Europe.[16] Unlike modernists, medievalists are provided with a limited number of texts which they must use to learn and interpret a millennium of history, culture, and literature. We learn to make the most of the bits and pieces that have come down to us and try to interpret the scanty evidence we have to decode and decipher a culture that will always remain alien from our own. Yet, to what extent should we treat the various texts that have been preserved for us on the same footing? For many years, a distinction was made between those texts—the works of Chaucer and Chrétien de Troyes, for example—that held aesthetic value from those that did not—for instance, *Bevis of Hampton*. Over the past few decades, thematic distinctions have gradually replaced aesthetic ones. Suzanne Conklin Akbari exemplifies this methodology in her *Idols in the East: European Representations of Islam and the Orient, 1100–1450*, whose primary goal is "to tease out the separate yet linked nature of religious and geographical alterity in the medieval discourse of Orientalism."[17] However, the texts with which Akbari engages, from Pierre d'Ailly's fifteenth-century *Imago Mundi* to the twelfth-century *chanson de geste Fierabras*, may be linked for us by their common medieval origin but may have received attention from very different quarters at the time of their com-

---

15 Whitaker, *Black Metaphors*, 191.

16 Maghan Keita, "Saracens and Black Knights," *Arthuriana*, 16, no. 4 (2006): 65.

17 Suzanne Conklin Akbari, *Idols in the East: European Representations of Islam and the Orient, 1100–1450* (Ithaca: Cornell University Press, 2009), 12.

position. How popular were d'Ailly's ideas amongst those interested neither in academic studies on geography nor in exploring the world? To what extent would a serf labouring the land, a merchant worried about the delay of his goods, or even an uneducated noblewoman have known about academic notions of geography in the period of the twelfth to the fifteenth centuries? Would the common approach to such issues have been similar to a cab driver's understanding of the Arthurian narrative today? If yes, what does this mean about our ability to pair such varied texts as popular *chansons de geste* with learned geographical treatises?

Thinking about our approach to medieval European works in this manner inevitably leads us to another distinction, one that is essential in thinking about the Othering of various peoples in the Middle Ages, namely the crucial difference between the realms of the imaginary and the historical. In the realm of the imagination, it is entirely possible for a black man to become white upon agreeing to baptism, as is the case in *The King of Tars*, or for a recent convert from Judaism to Christianity to be wholly accepted and assimilated into his or her new community. That I deal primarily with the imaginary makes it possible for me to speak both of medieval anxiety about Otherness and the erasure of that troubling Otherness: while some literary works present Otherness as changeable, others emphasize its permanency. Typically, those texts that conclude with the climactic conversion of an important figure—for example, a Saracen prince known for harassing Christians—appear to suggest that Otherness can be effaced and that the Other can become a true Christian. By contrast, those works that highlight the continued difference of the Other post conversion are dominated by anxiety about Otherness. Reading and discussing medieval literature deludes us into conceiving of medieval Europe as a time and place filled both with prejudice but also with possibility for those willing to convert. It is, therefore, sobering for students of literature such as myself to find out that conversion sometimes took place minutes before the execution of a member of an oppressed community, such as in the case of Mandl in the opening paragraph of this chapter. Not only was assimilation not certain in Mandl's case, but it was, in fact, neither possible nor even attempted. Mandl was coerced to convert so he could die a little less painfully. He was never expected to live and become a part of the Christian *communitas*.

The case of Mandl brings us to one more aspect of the debate about race and medieval Europe which must remain uppermost as we deal with the issue, namely that there existed some very real differences between different groups and communities represented as Other in medieval European texts. Akbari's *Idols in the East* again exemplifies the trend amongst some scholars to discuss the representation of Muslims alongside that of Jews in Western Europe in the Middle Ages. Yet, there were significant differences in the actual treatment of members of these groups. Although medieval Europeans may not necessarily have felt any compunction to treat Muslims better than Jews, to home in on two such "Othered" groups, Muslims were mostly removed from the nefarious repercussions of the "medieval discourse of Orientalism."[18] With the important exceptions of Iberia and the Syro-Palestinian region, where such discourse could and did have ter-

---

18 Akbari, *Idols in the East*, 12.

rifying repercussions for Jews and Muslims alike, Muslims did not suffer directly from medieval European ideas about them. The same, of course, could not be said of Jews in any part of medieval Western Europe, and England provides the earliest example of the extent to which such Othering, dehumanizing discourses can lead. As one of my first-year students put it recently, "The Muslims had a whole other world over there, but the Jews couldn't go anywhere!"[19] The Othering of Muslims in medieval Europe existed primarily within the realm of the imaginary. That of the Jews, by contrast, inhabited both imaginary and historical realms, the feverish imaginings of anti-Judaic tracts bleeding into legal antisemitism and massacres.

In one sense, this study is very much about race in the Middle Ages; yet it is also first and foremost about conversion. Conversion is inextricably intertwined with the emergence of the concept of race in medieval European culture and society. At a time when religion played such an important role in the lives of individuals, families, and societies, we can perceive race as having superseded religion in approaching the Other only when conversion is no longer recognized as a transformative experience. Only when baptism and conversion no longer have the power to alter the very physical, material essence of the individual who has chosen Christianity is it possible for the concept of race, with its emphasis on an essential, bodily difference that can never be removed or changed in any meaningful manner, to become the dominant mode by which medieval Europeans understand their world and categorize themselves and others within it. For this reason, the book uses conversion as a vehicle for navigating race and race-making in late medieval England.

The process by which racial difference displaces religious difference as the principal way of approaching new groups and cultures, however, is a gradual one, and my goal in the following chapters is to examine one very specific moment in the development of late medieval English literature when fascination with the Muslim Other and anxiety over the question of conversion competed for dominance in works focusing on interaction with the Muslim world. To explore this episode in medieval English literary history, I discuss several late texts that highlight individual journeys, potential or realized, from one religion to another. These narratives reveal fear of Christian conversion to another faith and emphasize, implicitly or explicitly, the possible failure of the Other's conversion to Christianity. In *Black Legacies: Race and the European Middle Ages*, Lynn Ramey repeatedly notes that "converts are surrounded by a miasma of doubt about the efficacy or completeness of their conversions."[20] What if the new convert was not sincere in his or her intentions? What if conversion is deployed as a tool to manipulate Christian forces into surrender or defeat? At the same time that these questions plague numerous works from the twelfth century onwards—pointing to a new interest in something

---

[19] I wish to thank Clara Fisher for this excellent summary of the crucial difference between the representation and treatment of Jews and Muslims in Western Europe in the Middle Ages.

[20] Lynn T. Ramey, *Black Legacies: Race and the European Middle Ages* (Gainesville: University Press of Florida, 2014), 31. Where Ramey alludes to medieval Europeans' conflicted attitudes towards conversion, I will attempt to identify a specific time when conversion comes to be perceived as a potential threat in late medieval England.

beginning to resemble the modern concept of race—much time and energy is spent imagining potential transitions from one "race-religion" to another.

The combined attraction and repulsion for an imaginary Muslim Other complicates narratives about Christian forays into the Muslim world. On the one hand, it is seen as frightening because it is different and not Christian; on the other hand, it is presented as wealthy and sometimes more welcoming than the Christian world, rendering it dangerously seductive to Christian heroes. This appeal goes beyond the characters inhabiting the narratives in question as poet after poet comes back to the same plot, imagining and re-imagining a fantasy Other whose difference is emphasized and highlighted only to be erased by narrative's end.[21] In the following pages, I will focus on two late medieval English narratives that depict the allure of the Muslim East while also stressing the potential dangers inherent to reliance on the conversion of the Other: the thirteenth-century legend ascribing a non-Christian mother to that most English of saints, St. Thomas Becket, and the much more famous *The Man of Law's Tale* from Geoffrey Chaucer's *Canterbury Tales*.

A Tale of Two Beckets: Becket's Mother and *The Man of Law's Tale*

The legend about Thomas Becket's non-Christian mother, a narrative I will refer to as the Becket legend, and *The Man of Law's Tale* make a good pair for several reasons. First, Chaucer's pilgrims are headed towards Thomas's shrine at Canterbury. Although Chaucer does not refer directly to the Becket legend in *The Canterbury Tales*, peripheral evidence suggests that Chaucer *did* know the stories about Gilbert Becket, Becket's father, and his pagan bride. To pair *The Man of Law's Tale* with the Becket legend thus allows us not only to juxtapose two narratives with important similarities, but also to discuss alongside *The Man of Law's Tale* a text that may well have served as a secondary source to the tale of Custance. At the very least, Chaucer can be seen as engaging and responding to the tale of Thomas Becket's legendary mother through *The Man of Law's Tale*. In addition to adding insight to late medieval English approaches to conversion and the Other, juxtaposing the legend with Chaucer's tale can thus illuminate the more famous of the two narratives, shedding new light on a well-known text.

At the same time—and paradoxically—that the Becket legend and *The Man of Law's Tale* can be seen as intricately linked, examining the tale alongside the legend, an obscure story whose ties to Chaucer's narrative have been mostly ignored by scholars until very recently, helps to de-familiarize *The Man of Law's Tale* and to wrench it from its usual, familiar context. Suzanne Conklin Akbari discusses the benefits of such de-familiarization in her recent essay, "Modeling Medieval World Literature," arguing for the juxtaposition of texts that do not necessarily bear any relationship to one another.[22] In this case, I concur with others who have argued that the tale responds to the Becket

---

21 The erasure of alterity, particularly in beautiful Saracen princesses, is one of the main themes of Jacqueline de Weever's *Sheba's Daughters*. Jacqueline de Weever, *Sheba's Daughters: Whitening and Demonizing the Saracen Woman in Medieval French Epic* (New York: Routledge, 2015).

22 Suzanne Conklin Akbari, "Modeling Medieval World Literature," *Middle Eastern Literatures*, 20, no. 1 (2017): 2–17.

legend. Yet, the juxtaposition of *The Man of Law's Tale* with the legend remains jarring because the legend is not one of the sources typically explored in attempting to understand the tale.

The Man of Law's Tale stands out in *The Canterbury Tales* as well as amongst other works dealing with the interaction between Latin Christendom and Islam. Whereas other late medieval texts present romantic love as a tool for the conversion of Muslims to Christianity, *The Man of Law's Tale* introduces its readers to that possibility only to dismiss it. In contrast to such works as *Bevis of Hampton* and *The King of Tars*, both briefly explored in chapter one, *The Man of Law's Tale* rejects the possibility of Muslim conversion through love and marriage. Not only is it the case that Custance's first marriage to the Sultan of Syria ends in a bloodbath that re-establishes the hegemony of the Islamic faith in Syria, but the story further proves that love *can* lead to the spread of Christianity when Custance's marriage to the pagan King Alla results in the conversion of Northumbria. *The Man of Law* here suggests that romantic love can lead to conversion but only for *some*. In the case of the Syrians, the *Man of Law* implies, love is simply not enough.

Juxtaposing *The Man of Law's Tale* with some of the earliest versions of the narrative describing Gilbert Becket's encounter with Thomas's heathen mother complicates this interpretation of the tale. Through the Man of Law, Chaucer appears to be playing with Thomas's legend, adding a preface to the preface to Thomas's story. In a retelling of the myth of *translatio imperii*, the transfer of power from Rome to England, Chaucer provides us with a prequel to Thomas's life that describes the spread of Christianity from Byzantium to England, one that mirrors the story of Thomas's conception and that allows the tradition about the saint's origin to come full circle. If Gilbert Becket facilitates the conversion of the non-Christian, Eastern princess who will become his wife and Thomas's mother, his faith is also rooted in the East, namely in the Byzantine princess that transmits Christianity to England.

Examining the narrative about Thomas's non-Christian mother likewise sheds new light on the Muslim characters, both good and bad, that inhabit *The Man of Law's Tale*. No mere foils to Alla and his English subjects, the Syrians arguably play a significant role in both the story of Custance and that of Thomas. The treasonous Syrians must retain their pagan law not only to enable the conversion of Alla and Northumberland but also to allow for the conception and birth of the woman who will conceive Thomas.

Yet, Chaucer's tale remains one of the starkest in its complete renunciation of any kind of rapprochement between the world of Islam and that of Latin Christendom. Unlike other High and late medieval narratives focusing, either partially or fully, on the Muslim world, *The Man of Law's Tale* refuses to give its audience the slightest hope in the conversion of the Muslim heathen, denying the Sultan those very tools—romantic love for a beautiful Christian woman—typically most useful in bringing a Muslim prince, for example the Sultan of Damascus in *The King of Tars*, to abjure his faith and seek Christian baptism. Where other, contemporaneous texts articulate the anxieties inherent to Muslim conversion to Christianity only to dismiss those fears when the Muslim villain or villainess becomes a true Christian, *The Man of Law's Tale* appears to legitimize his contemporaries' concerns, transforming the nightmare scenario of a new convert's betrayal into a horrifying reality. In this way, the tale both responds to and diverges strikingly from other pieces—including the Becket legend—dealing with the Muslim world in this period.

Before turning to the two narratives at the heart of this study, *The Man of Law's Tale* and the Becket legend, I will begin by contextualizing these two narratives within a larger tradition of representing the Muslim Other in literature of the High and late Middle Ages, focusing on the manner in which the conversion of important Muslim characters is treated in these texts. In this first chapter, I will look especially closely at two fourteenth-century Middle English works dealing with the conversion of a Muslim prince (or princess), *The King of Tars* and *Bevis of Hampton*. I argue that these two works part from other, earlier narratives underscoring the significance of Muslim conversion to Christianity—for example, the *Prise d'Orange*—by representing conversion as a long process connected with specific cultural, linguistic, and social mores rather than equating it with the singular act of baptism. This journey can take years, even decades, as is the case with the conversion of the Armenian princess Josian in *Bevis of Hampton*.

Having provided a frame of reference for the two narratives on which I focus in the rest of the study, I shift to the Becket legend in the second chapter. Because the Becket legend is by far the more obscure and less familiar of the two texts I examine, chapter two provides an overview of the earliest medieval versions of the legend, comparing and contrasting the various iterations of the narrative to each other and to historical accounts of the saint's parentage. Although there exist several later versions of this legend, the present study concentrates exclusively on the earliest, medieval versions of the narrative, especially those found in or derived from the Latin life of Becket known as The Later Quadrilogus or the Middle English *The South English Legendary*. As the two principal and most widely circulated medieval versions of the legend, these two texts are crucial to understanding the development of the saint's fabulous origin story. Chapter two ends by examining the manner in which the conversion of Becket's mother and her assimilation into urban London society is treated in the legend.

In chapters three and four, I turn to Chaucer's *Man of Law's Tale*. Concerned with the tale alone, chapter three is divided into two main sections. In the first half of the chapter, I describe the subtle, yet meaningful connections linking the tale with the Becket legend, emphasizing similarities between the two narratives and describing the influence of the legend on Chaucer's retelling of Trivet's story of the exiled but virtuous Christian princess Constance in *The Anglo-Norman Chronicles*. The rest of the chapter explores the manner in which conversion is dealt with and represented in the tale, looking both at the botched conversion of the Syrians and Custance's much more successful missionary endeavors in Northumbria.[23]

Chapter four likewise investigates *The Man of Law's Tale*, drawing on the previous chapter's discussion while examining the place and function of the tale within *The Canterbury Tales* as a whole. Once again divided into two halves, the chapter begins by re-

---

23 Throughout the rest of the study, I will use Chaucer's spelling for the name of his heroine to distinguish his particular adaptation of the tale and its primary character from any of the other versions of the Constance narrative circulating in the late Middle Ages.

opening the much-debated question of the relationship between the tale and its teller before exploring *The Man of Law's Tale* in the wider context of *The Canterbury Tales*. In doing so, I focus particularly on the *Endlink* and the connection this brief piece exposes between the Man of Law and the Parson, speculating as to the implications of the linkage between the two pilgrims for the treatment of conversion in *The Man of Law's Tale* and the collection as a whole.

Finally, my conclusion summarizes the study's main arguments on the changing approach to and representation of conversion in the fourteenth-century works discussed, *The Man of Law's Tale* and the Becket legend but also *The King of Tars* and *Bevis of Hampton*. Here, I conclude that the diminishing interest in conversion outlined in this study does not take place quickly and that its manifestation is not always consistent, much later works attesting to the persistence of the belief in conversion as the primary means of erasing alterity in medieval England. Although not all late medieval English texts reveal the type of ambivalence about conversion noted in the Becket legend and *The Man of Law's Tale*, this more ambiguous, far less enthusiastic response to the missionary ideal of conversion reveals, I will argue, a shift towards the racialization of the Muslim Other. The threat implicit in narratives such as the Becket legend suggests that there is something inherently and essentially different about Muslims and that socio-cultural factors such as customs, dress, and language do not simply vanish at the moment of baptism. Over the course of the fourteenth century, from the Becket legend to *The Man of Law's Tale*, this fear blossoms from a latent anxiety into a fully-fledged nightmare vision of insincere baptism as Christian bloodbath. The final chapter ends by indicating some possible new directions for further scholarship on the question of race and racialization in late medieval England.

A Note on Terminology

So far, I have referred to the Other described in many late medieval romances and *chansons de geste* as specifically *Muslim*. In fact, the pagan Other presented as a negative foil to the Christian hero(es) in such literary artifacts is not necessarily Muslim. Even when a character is identified as Saracen, a term equated by many scholars with "Muslim," or described as originating from an area historically acknowledged as Muslim, there can be no certainty that the work's audience is indeed meant to identify said character with Islam. Moreover, several texts do not use the label "Saracen," preferring instead to refer to the non-Christian prince or princess as "pagan" or "heathen." That medievalists use the terms "Saracen" and "Muslim" interchangeably, even when the text does not warrant such equation, raises crucial questions about the potency of unconscious prejudices.

Recent scholarship has highlighted the importance of terminology in texts focusing on Christian interaction with non-Christians, particularly when the Other seems to hail from the Muslim world. In "The Depoliticized Saracen and Muslim Erasure," Shokoofeh Rajabzadeh calls on medievalists to refer to the Saracens of medieval romances and *chansons de geste* as Muslims.[24] To do otherwise, Rajabzadeh argues, is to "depoliticize

---

24 Shokoofeh Rajabzadeh, "The Depoliticized Saracen and Muslim Erasure," *Literature Compass* 16 (2019): 1–8.

and delegitimize the violent and painful Islamophobia and racism of objects of study concerning Muslim representation."[25] Rajabzadeh uses the work of Geraldine Heng and Katherine Scarfe Beckett to underscore that the term "Saracen" is not merely a misnomer for Muslims but also that it displays, in and of itself, Islamophobia by presenting Muslims as shamefully and deceitfully trying to trace their biblical lineage to Sarah, the lawful wife of Abraham who eventually births Isaac, rather than Hagar, the bondswoman and mother of Ishmael.[26] She contends that "Saracen" refers to individuals neither historical nor fictional but is specifically used with the object of "(mis)representing Muslims."[27] And she concludes that "when we choose Saracen over Muslim, we look past the real Muslim whose body is translated on the page. The implications are that we present a version of the literature of the Middle Ages where Muslims were never present; they were always only imagined."[28]

Yet, using the term "Muslim" is not without risks. To use "Muslim" to refer to the Saracens of medieval literature only legitimizes the contemporary racism and Islamophobia Rajabzadeh decries at the beginning and end of her piece. By linking the fantastical imaginings of medieval Western European authors with hate crimes perpetrated in the twenty-first century, Rajabzadeh roots modern racist and Islamophobic ideology in the medieval past, thereby creating a lineage and tradition for modern acts of brutality and violence and, to a degree, justifying the perpetrators. How can any one individual repress their anti-Muslim conditioning when it issues from an ideology with such a long history?

At the same time, Rajabzadeh's piece is necessary precisely because it calls our attention to the modern stereotypes and preconceptions we might unconsciously be projecting and imposing onto the past. Rajabzadeh repeatedly cites contemporary medieval scholars who use the term "Saracen" in their discussion of texts that do not use that word or do not use it consistently.[29] Anyone who has spent some amount of time with medieval works will probably recall feeling puzzled by the translator's assurance that characters given a generic label are actually Saracens. The need for scholars to address such characters as Saracens, even when their identity in the text is ambiguously or unclearly stated, points to the assumption that medieval Europeans viewed the world just as we do and that medieval Europeans had a broad understanding of which peoples adhered to which faiths. In fact, this was not always the case as can be seen, for example, in *Bevis of Hampton*, where the Armenian king and his subjects are not Christians but Saracens.

Rajabzadeh's piece raises other important questions. For example, if the term "Saracen" is sometimes used to refer to peoples without the Muslim world, even if only occasionally, then what is the relationship between historical Muslims and the Saracens of the medieval European imaginary? To what extent did most medieval Europeans associate literary Saracens with real Muslims? What function did the Saracens of romances

---

25 Rajabzadeh, "The Depoliticized Saracen," 2.
26 Rajabzadeh, "The Depoliticized Saracen," 2–3.
27 Rajabzadeh, "The Depoliticized Saracen," 5.
28 Rajabzadeh, "The Depoliticized Saracen," 5.
29 Rajabzadeh, "The Depoliticized Saracen," 4, 5.

and *chansons de geste* play in the medieval European world view? In the chapters that follow, my goal is to be as faithful to the original narratives as possible and to use only the term(s) utilized in the texts themselves. In the case of the legend about Becket's mother, the development of the narrative underscores the fluidity of the term "Saracen" at the same time that it complicates the desire to equate "Saracen" with "Muslim." Just as we must rethink centuries-old assumptions and conventions about the relationship between medieval Europe and the rest of the world, so must we try to penetrate Europe's complicated approach to the Muslim world in the Middle Ages.

For medieval Europeans did understand their world very differently from us. Medieval Europeans believed not only that giants inhabited Saracen lands, but also that the miraculous intercession of a saint could heal the sick and infirm and that baptism could transform a lump of flesh into a healthy infant boy.[30] To discern the depths of medieval prejudice, it is first necessary to allow for, acknowledge, and accept such fundamental differences in thinking. Likewise, it is essential to understand that manifesting prejudice along such alternate modes of thinking in no way diminishes medieval intolerance and discrimination. The conundrum faced by Heng, Rajabzadeh, and multiple others debating the existence of racial elements in medieval texts lies in finding a way to impress the potency and tenacity of medieval Othering practices while simultaneously conveying the difference inherent to medieval thinking, tantalizingly close to ours, yet also forever remote and alien.

---

30 In *The King of Tars*, the Christian princess gives birth to a lump of flesh that miraculously transforms into a perfectly healthy child upon baptism. As to miraculous healing, the pile of crutches said to have been visible at the site of Thomas Becket's martyrdom in Canterbury bears testimony to the faith of medieval pilgrims.

Chapter 1

ANXIETIES OF CONVERSION IN HIGH AND LATE MEDIEVAL LITERATURE

Before turning to the Becket legend and Chaucer's *Man of Law's Tale*, some literary contextualization is necessary. What does conversion look like in other High and late medieval texts and how are converts from Islam to Christianity dealt with in these narratives? In order to understand where the Becket legend and *The Man of Law's Tale* stand in relationship to contemporary and near-contemporary works, this first chapter is dedicated to examining the place of conversion in four medieval poems and the concerns and questions raised in these pieces.

The chapter is divided in two main parts. In the first, I begin with that most ubiquitous of medieval texts, the *Chanson de Roland*, before exploring a later twelfth-century French narrative, the *Prise d'Orange*, both of which—to varying degrees—associate the Saracen Other with blackness and display unease about Saracens claiming to seek baptism. In the second half of the chapter, I turn to two late Middle English poems, *The King of Tars* and *Bevis of Hampton*, works produced by the same culture and society as that which engendered the Becket legend. These two pieces also arguably place more emphasis than the two twelfth-century French *chansons de geste* on the risks inherent to conversion. While *The King of Tars* suggests that conversion can pose a threat to the Christian community by allowing Christians to convert to other faiths, *Bevis of Hampton* further investigates this dangerous possibility. Perhaps even more importantly, *Bevis of Hampton* reveals that assimilation does not necessarily follow upon conversion and that baptism is only one of many necessary changes that herald a new beginning for the convert and his or her new community. In choosing these four texts, I provide both a general view of the treatment of conversion—and attendant anxieties—and a more specific overview of the subject in late medieval English works.

Several scholars have remarked on the anxieties associated with conversion in High and late medieval texts focusing on interactions with non-Christians. Sharon Kinoshita, for example, has noted that the *Chanson de Roland* underscores Christian suspicions of Saracens claiming to seek baptism.[1] Meanwhile, in *The Invention of Race in the European Middle Ages*, Geraldine Heng shows that converted Jews were essentialized and set apart from other Christians in thirteenth-century England, providing an interesting historical counterpart to Kinoshita's discussion of the subject.[2] Unlike the work of Kinoshita and Heng, however, the next few pages examine not general illustrations of Latin Christian anxiety about the conversion of the Other(s), but a very specific manifestation of that anxiety, namely the concern with socio-cultural factors such as dress,

---

[1] For more on Christian suspicion of Saracen conversion in the *Chanson de Roland*, see Sharon Kinoshita, "'Pagans are wrong and Christians are right': Alterity, Gender, and Nation in the *Chanson de Roland*," *Journal of Medieval and Early Modern Studies*, 31, no. 1 (2001): 85.

[2] Heng, *The Invention of Race*, 76–77.

customs, and language both before and *after* conversion to Christianity.[3] Such factors become increasingly significant in delineating Christians from non-Christians from the *Chanson de Roland* to *Bevis of Hampton*, from early twelfth-century France to fourteenth-century England. In arguing for the growing significance of these narrative elements, I look at three different stages on the path to conversion: 1) how difference is inscribed in the text; 2) the manner in which anxiety over the conversion of the Other manifests itself in the text; and 3) whether and how the text displays any anxiety over the new convert's assimilation after baptism. The later the text, the more likely it becomes that the kind of language and dress attributed to a character comes to play a role that is complementary—if not equal—to baptism in assessing his or her place in Christian society.

La Chanson de Roland

Perhaps the most famous of *chansons de geste*, the early twelfth-century *Chanson de Roland*, provides an intriguing example of an early work treating difference and conversion. The *Chanson de Roland* both remarks upon difference and approaches the possibility of Saracen conversion to Christianity with apprehension. Difference is noted briefly in the description of Frankish and Saracen troops. While the Franks hail from various parts of Western Europe, they are implicitly presented as white-skinned. In contrast, a few of the Saracen troops are explicitly described as dark-skinned, their blackness viewed as a signifier of evil as well as paramount ugliness. When Roland notices a group of black Saracens approaching towards him, the very sight of blackness confirms his worst fears about the rearguard's ultimate fate:

> Quan Rollant veit la contredite gent
> Ki plus sunt neirs que nen est arrement,
> Ne n'unt de blanc ne mais que sul les denz,
> Ço dist li quens: "Or sai jo veirement
> Que hoi murrum, par le mien escïent.
> Ferez, Franceis, car jo·l vos recumenz!"[4]

> When Rolland sees the accursed people,
> Who are blacker than ink
> And whose teeth alone are white,
> The Count said: "Now I know for certain
> That today we shall surely die.
> Strike, Frenchmen, for I am attacking again!"

Paula Gilbert Lewis notes that such passages cannot help but recall illustrations of modern racism.[5]

---

3 Jeffrey Jerome Cohen likewise emphasizes the importance of such factors: "Race is evinced in such highly visible actions as the choice, preparation and consumption of food; patterns of speech and use of language; law; customs and ritual; and practice of sexuality." Cohen, "Race," 112.
4 Gerard J. Brault, trans., *La Chanson de Roland* (University Park: Pennsylvania University Press, 1984), lines 1932–37.
5 Paula Gilbert Lewis, "The Contemporary Relevance of the Teaching of *La Chanson de Roland*: The Christian European Mind versus 'The Other,'" *College Language Association Journal*, 25, no. 3

Uncomfortable as these moments are, however, it is important to note that the equation between blackness and evil found in the *Chanson de Roland* does not necessarily imply a modern racist ideology descrying blackness as a signifier of intellectual and social inferiority. Geraldine Heng emphasizes the importance of distinguishing between different kinds of blackness in medieval literature:

> In contemplating epidermal race, it is thus useful to recognize a distinction between *hermeneutic blackness* in which exegetical considerations are paramount and often explicitly foregrounded, and *physiognomic blackness linked to the characterization of black Africans* in phenomena that extended beyond immediate theological exegesis.[6]

The representation of black Saracens in the *Chanson de Roland* and the extremely negative description of black Saracen troops may be read as exemplifying Heng's concept of "*hermeneutic blackness*," in which individuals are painted black and described pejoratively as a way to underscore their sinfulness and lack of virtue.

Aside from the ambiguous meaning of blackness in the *Chanson de Roland*, the difference the black Saracen troops embody also plays a very minor role in the poem. If anything, as Sharon Kinoshita notes, "each camp, as critics inevitably note, is in fact a mirror image of the other."[7] Both Christian and Saracen leaders hold counsel with their barons at the beginning of the poem, both groups privilege twelve warriors that surpass all of their companions, Christians and Saracens use similar calls when charging into battle—the list goes on and on. As Kinoshita shows in "'Pagans are wrong and Christians are right': Alterity, Gender, and Nation in the *Chanson de Roland*," there is in fact far too much similarity and *likeness* between Christians and Saracens in the *Chanson de Roland*, the only true difference dividing the two camps—and it is a crucial one—being faith. Thus, it seems that blackness as difference is introduced only to be subsumed under the far more significant element of the Saracens' alien faith. Heng's label, "*hermeneutic blackness*," seems most appropriate in approaching those few Saracen troops described as black, their skin colour meant to confirm the evil of the Saracen religion and, by implication, the truth of Christianity.

As for Christian anxiety about conversion, the issue initially appears central to the work. The first fifteen laisses of the poem deal with the Saracen King Marsile's attempt to deceive Charlemagne by promising to embrace Christianity as soon as the emperor has left Spain. Of course, the king's projected conversion never comes to fruition, and Marsile's false promises mutate into armed combat between Christians and Saracens. However, the conflict is overshadowed by the deception of the Christian baron Ganelon, and it is the trial of Ganelon that occupies the rest of the poem. The text's initial focus on the dangers inherent to the conversion of the Other to Christianity thus turns into a red herring.

One conversion does take place in the *Chanson de Roland*, that of Marsile's queen, Bramimonde. As the tale of Roland's bravery and Ganelon's treachery unfolds, the audi-

---

(March 1982): 344–45, as quoted in Kinoshita, "'Pagans are wrong and Christians are right,'" 82.
6 Heng, *The Invention of Race*, 185.
7 Kinoshita, "'Pagans are wrong and Christians are right,'" 83.

ence bears witness to Bramimonde's gradual renunciation of the Saracen faith. For this pivotal character, the need to convert arises out of the powerlessness of the Saracen idols, deaf to her pleas for help.[8] At the very end of the narrative, Charlemagne acknowledges that Bramimonde needs to be taught Christianity, presumably to convert for positive as well as negative reasons: Bramimonde must embrace Christianity on its own merits rather than simply to evade the false and useless Saracen faith. For this, Charlemagne plans to have her converted "through love," a goal the bishops of France hope to accomplish through the intermediary of noble godmothers who will instruct the queen of Spain about her new faith.[9]

This last detail not only sets Bramimonde's conversion against that of her subjects forced to choose between baptism and death, but also hints at the possibility that gender plays a role in the treatment of the Saracen queen. Although Bramimonde seeks baptism of her own free will, she needs to be feminized. At the court of Marsile, she has played a masculine role—she is, for instance, an active participant in the negotiations of Ganelon's betrayal at the opening of the poem—and Charlemagne both acknowledges and attempts to rectify Bramimonde's lack of proper gender performance by tacitly agreeing that it will be *godmothers* who will instruct the queen about her new faith.[10] In "'Pagans are wrong and Christians are right'," Kinoshita compellingly argues against reading the *Chanson de Roland* as a masculine warrior epic by emphasizing the crucial role played by Bramimonde. Rather than relegating the women of the *Chanson de Roland* to the margins of the story, Kinoshita advocates that the women serve as the only non-religious site of difference between Christians and Saracens, allowing audiences to distinguish between the two groups when the two in fact share so much that their lack of difference might otherwise cause unease.[11] Unlike the men, the women react to death and loss in radically different ways: where Aude rejects the possibility of life without Roland, Bramimonde learns not only to live without Marsile but also to substitute the Christian God for her false Saracen deities.[12] As Kinoshita puts it, "If Aude's ideological task is to refuse all exchange, Bramimonde's is to embrace it."[13]

In the end, it is Bramimonde's baptism that serves as the climactic event of the poem. The text does not allow any room for speculation about Bramimonde's place in Frankish society once she has converted, and we are left to assume that assimilation into Latin Christendom will follow immediately upon conversion. Where the poem opened on deep anxieties about Saracen conversion to Christianity, it ends with a complete lack of concern for Bramimonde's assimilation into Frankish society after baptism. Rather, we are to take for granted that the Saracen queen will vanish to be replaced immediately and fully by a Christian woman.

---

8 *Chanson de Roland*, laisses 187 and 195, for example.
9 *Chanson de Roland*, laisse 272, line 3674 and laisse 297, lines 3978–83 respectively.
10 See *Chanson de Roland*, laisse 50 for Bramimonde's interaction with Ganelon at Marsile's court.
11 Kinoshita, "'Pagans are wrong and Christians are right.'"
12 Sharon Kinoshita, *Medieval Boundaries: Rethinking Difference in Old French Literature* (Philadelphia: University of Pennsylvania Press, 2006), 43.
13 Kinoshita, *Medieval Boundaries*, 43.

La Prise d'Orange

In the *Prise d'Orange*, composed around the middle of the twelfth century, difference is marked much more strongly than in the *Chanson de Roland*.[14] As with the earlier work, the Saracen villains look different from the Christian heroes. Unlike the *Chanson de Roland*, however, physical difference, once again equated primarily with blackness, does not simply appear on a few of the Saracen battalions. Rather, blackness constitutes one of two primary markers of the Saracen faith in the *Prise d'Orange* and serves to distinguish Christians from Saracens. As a result, much emphasis is placed on the need for Guillaume, the text's hero, and his men to paint their faces black in order to pass as Saracens.[15] The Christians succeed in deceiving the Saracens until a tunic of gold is flung at Guillaume's face, removing the black dye and revealing him to be white.[16]

Although the differentiation of Christians from Saracens along colour lines hints at the racialization of both groups in the poem, the Saracens' blackness again appears rooted in a hermeneutic approach to the Other. Guillaume's blackface performance suggests that the text's narrative logic is based on the belief that Saracens are black and evil and Christians white and good. According to this interpretation, the seemingly essential blackness of William's Saracen foe reflects their sins and evil nature rather than marking them racially. The Saracens' blackness and the sins and negative attributes that blackness connotes reflect the lack of divine grace in their lives, a physical indicator of their spiritual deficiency.

Likewise, the fact that the Saracen princess Orable, the work's heroine and Guillaume's lover, is white reinforces the argument that skin colour reflects a character's inner virtue—or lack thereof—in the *chanson*. Orable's whiteness is emphasized repeatedly in the text, for example at lines 205, 278, 665, and 1226. Jacqueline de Weever and Lynn Tarte Ramey have both remarked on Orable's white skin, De Weever arguing that the colour of her skin "nullifies Orable's alterity" and Ramey stating that Orable's whiteness renders her suspicious to the Saracens even before her betrayal of her kin on behalf of Guillaume and his companions.[17] Valentina Jones-Wagner makes a larger argument that the potential for conversion is inscribed on the body of the white Saracen princess.[18] Unlike the other Saracens, Orable's whiteness signals her readiness to adopt Christianity. Skin colour, then, performs a symbolic function in the *Prise d'Orange*, both illustrating inherent virtue and emphasizing a character's capacity to embrace the one true faith.

Unlike in the *Chanson de Roland*, however, skin colour is not the only distinguishing factor between Christians and Saracens in the *Prise d'Orange*, and language is portrayed

---

[14] Joan Ferrante, ed. and trans., introduction to *Guillaume d'Orange: Four Twelfth-Century Epics* (New York: Columbia University Press, 1974), 15.

[15] *Prise d'Orange*, lines 375–80 and 451–52, for instance.

[16] *Prise d'Orange*, lines 774–78.

[17] De Weever, *Sheba's Daughters*, 24–25; Lynn Tarte Ramey, "Role Models? Saracen Women in Medieval French Epic," *Romance Notes*, 41, no. 2 (2001): 138.

[18] Valentina Jones-Wagner, "The Body of the Saracen Princess in *La Belle Helene de Constantinople*," *Bucknell Review*, 47, no. 2 (2004): 86.

as an important secondary factor in distinguishing Christians from Saracens.[19] The essential nature of language in differentiating one group from another becomes apparent as Guillaume prepares to infiltrate Orange. Knowing that one of his men, Gilbert, learned the Saracen language during his long captivity at the hands of the enemy, he coaxes and wheedles Gilbert into accompanying him on his foray into Orange to try and capture the city and win Orable's love.[20]

If language is important in determining whether one belongs in the Christian or the Saracen camp, however, the text is somewhat inconsistent in highlighting the linguistic difference separating Christian heroes from Saracen foes. When Guillaume and his two companions, Gilbert and Guielin, first arrive in Orange, we are reminded that only Gilbert can speak both languages when he is sent to speak to the porter alone.[21] Later, however, the Saracen prince Aragon, Orable's stepson, engages in direct communication with Guillaume, as if there existed no language barrier between the two men.[22] Yet, when Guillaume finally meets Orable, she tells him that she is "versed in your tongue" perhaps the further to underscore her ability to transgress the boundaries of her birth community and assimilate into a new socio-religious system.[23]

Despite—or perhaps because of—the existence of not one, but two clear markers of difference in the *Prise d'Orange*, the narrative betrays much more anxiety about conversion than does the *Chanson de Roland*. Even though Orable arms Guillaume and his two companions, Gilbert and Guielin, when Guillaume's disguise is unveiled, Guielin immediately jumps to the conclusion that Orable has betrayed them after Aragon attacks the three Christian men.[24] Guillaume himself echoes Guielin's suspicions about the white, multilingual queen less than two hundred lines later.[25] Even more interesting, perhaps, is the fear voiced about Gilbert at the end of the narrative when Gilbert has to lead Guillaume's nephew Bertrand through a secret cave and tunnel so as to facilitate the rescue of Guillaume, Guielin, and Orable and allow for the Christian capture of Orange. Because Gilbert leads Bertrand and his men through dark, hidden passageways, the latter concludes that Gilbert has reneged his Christian faith and betrayed his former companions.[26]

These three instances in which the text articulates fear about conversion in the *Prise d'Orange* are especially enlightening in the manner in which they diverge from the anxieties about conversion expressed at the very beginning of the *Chanson de Roland*. Where the primary concern about the conversion of the Other to Christianity in the *Chanson de Roland* lies in the suspicion that the Saracens could use conversion as a tool to manipulate Charlemagne and his men, the *Prise d'Orange* reveals anxiety not only about the

---

[19] Kinoshita, "'Pagans are wrong and Christians are right,'" 106n19.
[20] *Prise d'Orange*, lines 320–27.
[21] *Prise d'Orange*, lines 418–19.
[22] *Prise d'Orange*, lines 568–69.
[23] *Prise d'Orange*, line 720.
[24] *Prise d'Orange*, lines 1188–89 and 1195–96.
[25] *Prise d'Orange*, lines 1356–57.
[26] *Prise d'Orange*, lines 1786–88.

sincerity of a new convert's faith, but also about a captive's potential to renounce his community of origin and turn to the faith of his captors. In the *Prise d'Orange*, conversion is perceived as a double-edged sword, one that can be used against Christians and lead to betrayal in a number of different ways.

In the end, however, all fears are cast aside as the *Prise d'Orange* concludes with the baptism of Orable and her marriage to Guillaume in what Kinoshita has seen as "an eroticized representation of Frankish aggression against the Saracens of Spain."[27] Once again, we are left with the image of a baptized woman for whom assimilation into the Christian *communitas* is not an issue for concern. In spite of a heightened sense of difference between Saracens and Christians and a lingering fear of betrayal by those like Orable and Gilbert who can move back and forth between worlds, languages, and cultures, the *Prise d'Orange* ends with a clear affirmation of Christian dominance, one that asserts the power of the Christian community to mold and re-shape the Saracen Orable into a Christian noblewoman.

The King of Tars

Other, later works both accentuate differentiating factors separating various groups and communities and magnify evolving anxieties about the conversion of non-Christians. To illustrate this point, I will focus on two late medieval English works, *The King of Tars* and *Bevis of Hampton*, narratives near-contemporaneous with the Becket legend and similar to it in their focus on the relationships—romantic and other—between Latin Christians and Saracens. In particular, *The King of Tars* is an important text to consider when discussing *The Man of Law's Tale* since it also belongs to the Constance-cycle.[28]

A growing body of scholarship has emerged on *The King of Tars* over the course of the past twenty years, much of it concerned with the intersection of race-making and religion in medieval Europe.[29] In "Marking Religion on the Body: Saracens, Categorization, and the King of Tars," for example, Siobhain Bly Calkin identifies the fear of interfaith sex and coupling as central to the work.[30] At the same time, Calkin notes that the text would resonate with English audiences struggling to make sense of their relationships both with the French and with the Scots in the fourteenth century.[31] Yet two other

---

27 Kinoshita, *Medieval Boundaries*, 73.

28 Sierra Lomuto, "The Mongol Princess of Tars: Global Relations and Racial Formation in *The King of Tars* (c. 1330)," *Exemplaria*, 31, no. 3 (2019): 182.

29 This body of scholarship includes, but is not limited to: Aman Y. Nadhiri, *Saracens and Franks in the 12th–15th Century European and Near Eastern Literature: Perceptions of Self and Other* (London: Routledge, 2017); Siobhain Bly Calkin, "Marking Religion on the Body: Saracens, Categorization, and the King of Tars," *Journal of English and Germanic Philology*, 104, no. 2 (2005): 219–38; Jamie Friedman, "Making Whiteness Matter: The King of Tars," *postmedieval*, 6, no. 1 (2015): 52–63; Lomuto, "The Mongol Princess of Tars," 171–92; Whitaker, *Black Metaphors*; Amy Burge, *Representing Difference in the Medieval and Modern Orientalist Romance* (Basingstoke: Palgrave, 2016).

30 Calkin, "Marking Religion on the Body," 219–38.

31 Calkin, "Marking Religion on the Body," 238.

scholars, Jamie Friedman and Sierra Lomuto, examine the work's heroine as a *Mongol* princess.[32] While Friedman argues that the text turns the king of Tars, a Mongol leader, and his daughter into "hyperversions of the Christian racial ideal" as a result of a contemporary obsession with the Mongols, Lomuto highlights that "the less visible, yet still present, racial formation of the Mongol figure drives the colonialist fantasy at the core of the romance."[33]

Indeed, *The King of Tars* provides an interesting alternative to the Saracen princess motif: unlike Bramimonde and Orable, the woman who converts at the beginning of *The King of Tars* is a Christian princess forced to convert to the Saracen law.[34] After initially rejecting both conversion and marriage to the Sultan of Damascus, the daughter of the king of Tars finally accepts to wed the sultan when the latter defeats her father in battle. When she arrives in Damascus, the princess is immediately attired in new clothing. In the Auchinleck manuscript, dating to the 1330s and considered by most editors as the most authoritative version of the poem, the princess's change of clothing signals a seemingly profound change of identity:[35]

> Into chaumber sche was ladde,
> And richeliche sche was cladde
> As hethen wiman ware.[36]

> Into a chamber she was led,
> And richly she was clad
> Like heathen women.[37]

In one of two later manuscripts of *The King of Tars*, the Vernon manuscript dated no earlier than 1380, the princess's change of clothes is described in even greater detail:[38]

> With riche clothes heo was cled
> Hethene as thaugh heo ware.
> The Soudan ther he sat in halle.
>
> He comaundede his knihtes alle
> That maiden for to fette.

---

[32] Friedman, "Making Whiteness Matter," 52–63; Lomuto, "The Mongol Princess of Tars," 171–92.

[33] Friedman, "Making Whiteness Matter," 54; Lomuto, "The Mongol Princess of Tars," 172–73. Lomuto also indicates that the basis of the story of a Mongol leader converting to Christianity as a result of the miraculous transformation of his infant child appears in the *Flores Historiarum* and several other historical sources predating *The King of Tars*. Lomuto, "The Mongol Princess of Tars," 178.

[34] As was the case with the *Chanson de Roland* and the *Prise d'Orange*, the term "Saracen" applies when discussing *The King of Tars*. The later narrative alternates interchangeably between the terms "hethen" and "Sarrazin" to refer to the Sultan and his followers. Throughout this study, I will be using John H. Chandler's 2015 edition of *The King of Tars* for TEAMS's Middle English Text Series. John H. Chandler, ed., *The King of Tars* (Kalamazoo: Medieval Institute Publications, 2015).

[35] John H. Chandler, "Introduction" to John H. Chandler, ed., *The King of Tars* (Kalamazoo: Medieval Institute Publications, 2015), 17.

[36] *King of Tars*, lines 379–81.

[37] All translations in this chapter are my own.

[38] Chandler, "Introduction," 19.

> In cloth of riche purpel palle,
> And on hire hed a comely calle,
> > Bi the Soudan heo was sette.[39]
>
> With rich clothes she was clad
> > As if she were heathen.
>
> The Sultan sat in his hall.
> He ordered all of his knights
> > To fetch that maiden.
> In cloth of rich purple pall,
> And on her head a pretty hood,
> > To the Sultan she was brought.

In all three manuscripts, the princess's transformation into a Saracen woman begins with her clothing. Having arrived at her Saracen husband's court, she is immediately changed into a new outfit, one that, according to the Auchinleck redactor(s), makes her look like the other heathen women. The compiler of the Vernon some fifty years later stresses that the clothes the princess now wears make her appear heathen, a subtle change giving added significance to the princess's dress. Where the earlier Auchinleck version depicts the princess of Tars as merely *looking* like heathen women, the later Vernon manuscript presents her as having become a heathen woman, at least in appearance. The sultaness's new clothes are described as beautiful in all three manuscripts, though the Vernon again provides more information. Whereas the Auchinleck and the Simeon versions simply describe the princess's clothing as luxurious, the Vernon emphasizes that the fabric is rich as well as coloured purple, the traditional colour of royalty.[40] Finally, the brief passage in the Vernon adds that the princess's attire is complemented by a headdress.

The princess's new costume symbolizes her apparent acceptance of her new life. As Amy Burge notes, the new clothes of the princess of Tars "indicate a particular religious affiliation," and this is especially noteworthy in the Vernon version of the tale.[41] From there to acceptance of a new belief system is but a short step, and when the sultan asks his bride if she will convert to his law, she states her firm intention to do so:

> "Sir, Y nil thee nought greve.
> > Teche me now and lat me here
> Hou Y schal make mi preiere
> > When ich on hem bileve.
> To Mahoun ichil me take
> And Jhesu Crist mi lord forsake,
> > That made Adam and Eve,
> And seththen serve thee at wille
> Arliche and lat, loude and stille,
> > A morwe and an eve."[42]

---

39 *King of Tars*, Vernon MS, lines 353–60.
40 The Simeon MS is dated to the same period as the Vernon MS. Chandler, "Introduction," 19.
41 Burge, *Representing Difference*, 123.
42 *King of Tars*, lines 480–89.

> "Sir, I will not grieve you.
>   Teach me now and let me hear
>   How I shall make my prayer
>   When I believe in them.
>
> On Mohammed I shall rely
> And Jesus Christ my lord forsake,
>   Who made Adam and Eve,
> And from then on I will serve you at will
> Early and late, loudly and quietly,
>   In the morning and in the evening."

In this startling declaration, the princess does not merely suggest herself to be open to the possibility of conversion to the sultan's faith but, rather, assures him that she will reject Christianity. The Christian heroine's overt adoption of the sultan's Saracen faith leads to, at best, religious ambiguity and, at worst, religious hybridity.[43] In Siobhain Bly Calkin's reading of this moment, "religious identity can no longer be clearly discerned and miscategorization occurs."[44] What initiates this troubling miscategorization is neither emotional, ideological, or spiritual weakness but simply clothing.

Interestingly, attention is given not only to clothing but also to the more practical aspects of conversion: although the princess's statement concludes with a more general and sweeping renunciation of Christianity, it begins with a request to the sultan to teach her how to pray. This opening plea, insincere as it might be, points to an interest in the practical, socio-cultural facets of conversion. How can an individual who has not been raised into his or her new faith know how to "make mi preiere / When ich on hem bileve"?[45]

The princess continues to observe her husband's Saracen faith publicly until she gives birth to a child described simply as an insensate "rond of flesche" (lump of flesh).[46] The lump-child's monstrous "indeterminacy" results from the disturbing interfaith union of its parents generally and its mother's apparent religious hybridity more specifically.[47] According to Calkin:

> The child of the unconverted Christian princess and her Saracen husband constitutes a being that unites Christian and Saracen identities and therefore defies religious identification. Theoretically, the child offers the possibility of no longer needing to concern oneself with religious categories and sociocultural differences since it conflates such categories and differences.[48]

A world without religious differentiation and categorization, Calkin argues, is both horrifying and unviable.[49]

---

[43] Burge, *Representing Difference*, 126.
[44] Calkin, "Marking Religion on the Body," 224.
[45] *King of Tars*, lines 482–83.
[46] *King of Tars*, line 577.
[47] Calkin, "Marking Religion on the Body," 228; Burge, *Representing Difference*, 126.
[48] Calkin, "Marking Religion on the Body," 226.
[49] Calkin, "Marking Religion on the Body," 227.

After the baptism and immediate transformation of the princess's newborn into a beautiful male heir, the sultan acknowledges the power and superiority of Christianity, and the false conversion of the beginning is paralleled with the much more positive conversion of the sultan. Before accepting Christian baptism, the sultan goes through a journey similar to that of Bramimonde in the *Chanson de Roland*, begging assistance from his idols before denigrating them for refusing to breathe life into his child.[50] The birth and subsequent transformation of the lump serves as a crucial turning point in the narrative.[51]

If the son of the sultan and the princess of Tars enjoys a double transformation, the shapeless lump becoming a beautiful, well-shaped child at the moment of his baptism, so does his father who undergoes a physical as well as a spiritual transformation upon embracing the Christian faith. Prior to the sultan's baptism, the only physical description given of him occurs upon the princess's arrival at his court: while his new bride dons luxurious Saracen clothes, the sultan himself serves as her negative foil, "so foule a mett" ("so foul a mate") for the beautiful, virtuous princess.[52] What that foulness entails remains a mystery until the sultan becomes receptive to the truth of Christianity. As he renounces his idols and witnesses the radical transformation of his child upon baptism, we finally learn that the sultan is, in fact, black.[53] Less than a hundred and fifty lines later, the sultan himself receives baptism. We are then given more details about his appearance, current and previous:

> His hide that blac and lothely was
> Al white bicom thurth Godes gras
> And clere withouten blame.[54]
>
> His skin that was black and loathly
> Became all white through God's grace
> And pure without flaw.

The blackness of the Sultan of Damascus's skin is thus not only presented as unappealing and ugly, but it is also associated with his hostility towards Christianity and Christian believers and, therefore, his lack of virtue and the sinfulness of his existence. The equation between white skin and spiritual virtue is further emphasized by the fact that the simple act of baptism has the immediate and unalloyed power to transform the sultan from a being both foul in appearance and lacking in essential virtues into a white man "clere withouten blame."

The sultan's blackness—and the negative connotations of that blackness in the text—further complexifies our approach to the Saracen Other in *The King of Tars* and raises important questions about the emergence of the concept of race. Several scholars, including Geraldine Heng and Lisa Lampert-Weissig, see the text as "focusing spe-

---

50 *King of Tars*, lines 634–57.
51 Lomuto, "The Mongol Princess of Tars," 187.
52 *King of Tars*, line 390.
53 *King of Tars*, line 793.
54 *King of Tars*, lines 922–24.

cifically on skin colour as a racial marker and how it comes to signify a delimiting line between Saracen and Christin identities."[55] Others, however, emphasize the complexity surrounding the sultan's transformation. While Calkin ultimately agrees with Heng and Lampert-Weissig that "The sultan's conversion and change of colour constitute...a moment when certain modern understandings and discussions of race intersect with a medieval text," she also stresses the porous nature of religious identification that necessitates such a stratagem as a last, desperate measure to establish a way to differentiate between Christian and Muslim in a world complicated by the possibility of conversion.[56] In Calkin's words:

> This fantasy emerges...in response to a lengthy series of events that illustrate both the possibility of miscategorizing individuals based on their physical appearance and the horror that ensues from failed categorization and differentiation.[57]

By contrast, Cord J. Whitaker expressly denies the racial implications of the sultan's transformation:

> The *King of Tars* exploits blackness and whiteness's associations with non-Christian sinfulness and Christian purity only to prove them erroneous. The text turns its reader's gaze away from physical skin color and toward the much harder to grasp significance of color in the realm of spiritual metaphor.[58]

To Whitaker, the simplistic transformation of the sultan from black to white upon conversion to Christianity is no more than a "rhetorical mirage" that deceives audiences into thinking that categorization is not only possible but easy when, in fact, the very opposite seems to be the case.[59]

In its dual concern with conversion and the distinction between believers and non-believers, *The King of Tars* has much in common with the *Prise d'Orange*. Just as in the earlier work, *The King of Tars* manifests clear and explicit anxiety about the possibility of Christians converting to the Saracen faith. As in the *Prise d'Orange* as well, *The King of Tars* uses skin colour to differentiate between Christians and non-Christians. Here again, the sin of the Saracen faith is inscribed upon non-Christian skin. Both texts also present conversion as consisting of a combination of socio-cultural behaviours—dress in *The King of Tars* and language in the *Prise d'Orange*—and skin colour. To convert, individuals must not only pledge themselves to their new faith and physically show they possess inherent virtue and spiritual worth, but they must also enact the behaviours and adopt the customs of the community associated with that faith.

Where the two texts diverge is in the value they assign to the modes of differentiation they privilege. Where skin colour is a *sine qua non* in the *Prise d'Orange*, stressing not only who possesses the virtue required to become Christian but also foreshadowing the conversion of those Saracens deemed worthy of the Christian faith, socio-cultural

---

55 Lomuto, "The Mongol Princess of Tars," 175.
56 Calkin, "Marking Religion on the Body," 231.
57 Calkin, "Marking Religion on the Body," 220.
58 Whitaker, *Black Metaphors*, 46.
59 Whitaker, *Black Metaphors*, 40.

practices such as dress and customs dominate over skin colour as a means of identification in *The King of Tars*. Skin colour in the later fourteenth-century work seems more of an afterthought than anything. No attention is paid to the Sultan's blackness—or that of any other character in the work—until that blackness is about to be erased. By contrast, the new, heathenish attire of the princess of Tars is foregrounded in the text, creating a deep unease about her spiritual state of being. If her disguise is so persuasive, to what extent can she herself resist the faith that has been thrust upon her? How long will it be before that disguise, one that signals the princess's successful ability to pass, encroaches upon her very heart and soul and turns her into a true heathen? How long, in short, can she wear the disguise without becoming the thing she is pretending to be?

The anxiety surrounding the princess's false conversion points to another place of divergence between the *Prise d'Orange* and *The King of Tars*. While the fear that Gilbert, another character marked as transgressive, might renege his Christian faith is only articulated at the very end of the *Prise d'Orange* and in passing, *The King of Tars* highlights the princess's problematic false conversion from the very beginning of the poem. A baptism still serves as the narrative's climactic event in *The King of Tars* but conversion appears to have become a much more complicated, much more threatening possibility in the roughly two hundred years since the composition of the *Prise d'Orange*.

Bevis of Hampton

Another early fourteenth-century work, the extremely popular English poem *Bevis of Hampton*, also deals extensively with conversion.[60] Rather than an event, powerful and miraculous though it might be, conversion is presented as a process in *Bevis of Hampton*. The text explores various kinds of conversion from the Saracen faith to Christianity and vice versa.

The need to explore conversion manifests itself fairly early on in *Sir Bevis of Hampton*. After Bevis's mother, the daughter of the king of Scotland, kills her husband and has Bevis sold into slavery, the boy is bought by the Saracen king Ermin of Arminia, who raises him and has him knighted. The narrative conveniently skips over much of Bevis's youth in Armenia, and we next encounter him at the age of fifteen, having come into the possession of the horse Arondel and quite comfortable in his Saracen surroundings. Despite having received a horse and training in the art of knighthood, Bevis displays no interest in returning to England and avenging his father's death, his stated goal only a few lines earlier. Rather, Siobhain Bly Calkin has argued, he "acts in ways that indicate a profound assimilation into the Saracen world of the text, and undermine his claim to be a model hero of medieval western romance."[61] In developing this argument, Calkin high-

---

60 In the introduction to the TEAMS edition of *Bevis of Hampton*—the edition I will be referring to throughout this section—the text is said to have been composed "(c. 1324)." Ronald B. Herzman, Graham Drake, and Eve Salisbury, "Introduction" to Ronald B. Herzman, Graham Drake, and Eve Salisbury, ed., *Bevis of Hampton* (Kalamazoo: Medieval Institute Publications, 1999), 187.

61 Siobhain Bly Calkin, "The Anxieties of Encounter and Exchange: Saracens and Christian Heroism in *Sir Beves of Hamtoun*," *Florilegium* 21 (2004): 135–58 at 138.

lights two episodes in particular: the hero's first battle and his exchange with his cousin while serving as a messenger for Ermin to King Brademond of Damascus.

The first of these two episodes, Bevis's first battle on Christmas Day, shows that our hero has not only forgotten his need to take revenge on his mother and stepfather but, far more importantly, what it means to be Christian.[62] In fact, his Saracen companions have to remind him that it is Christmas Day. Although they laugh at his ignorance, Bevis's Saracen fellows otherwise convey a message of religious tolerance. Unlike Saracens in other works dealing with the encounter between Latin Christendom and Islam, they do not belittle the Christian hero or assert the superiority of their faith over his. Rather, they enjoin Bevis to stay as true to his god as they are to theirs.[63] Bevis, however, cannot grasp this message: the Saracens' words bring him shame because they remind him that he has lost his way as a Christian son dedicated to the pursuit of his father's killer. When he responds to the man who first mentioned Christmas, he evokes his father before resorting to language so aggressive that a battle quickly follows, one in which he kills all of his Saracen companions.

This episode is strange in many ways: Bevis is amongst friends, and the words that begin the massacre of the Saracens could be read as gentle banter if not even a lighthearted attempt on the Saracens' part to acknowledge and show their acceptance of their peer's difference.[64] Why then must Bevis respond so aggressively? In part, I would argue, the problem lies precisely in Bevis's lack of conflict in Armenia. Where his Christian brethren—including his mother—treated him terribly in his native England, Bevis initially encounters nothing but love and support at Ermin's court. Bevis must fight and kill Saracens at this juncture to show that he remains true to Christianity despite the allure and seduction of a world that has treated him with kindness and respect. In describing the woes of Bevis in his native land and his ease and comfort at the Saracen king's court, the poem's anonymous composer creates a situation where Bevis's conversion to the Saracen faith seems inevitable. For all of Bevis's earlier talk about his father and his desire for revenge, his Christian, European upbringing seems to have receded into the background. In the words of Linda Lomperis, Bevis can no longer distinguish between "[c]ategories of 'home' and 'not home'."[65] Like the narrator of *The Travels of Sir John Mandeville*, Bevis has learned both to pass and to enjoy passing.[66] Life at the Saracen court of King Ermin has transformed Bevis into "someone who plays a part so well that he...effectively becomes the part, someone, in other words, who, Hamlet-like, renders as natural that which is merely performance."[67] In the process, Bevis seems momentarily to have lost his hold on his Christian

---

62 *Bevis of Hampton*, lines 585–642.

63 *Bevis of Hampton*, line 605.

64 Helen Young, *Constructing "England" in the Fourteenth Century: A Postcolonial Interpretation of Middle English Romance* (Lewiston: Edwin Mellen, 2010), 147.

65 Linda Lomperis, "Medieval Travel Writing and the Question of Race," *Journal of Medieval and Early Modern Studies*, 31, no. 1 (Winter 2001): 150.

66 Lomperis, "Medieval Travel Writing," 156.

67 Lomperis, "Medieval Travel Writing," 153.

identity.[68] But Bevis is no renegade, and his murder of his Saracen companions on Christmas Day proves this—by this point in the narrative—somewhat contentious claim.[69]

This resounding affirmation of Bevis's Christian faith is undermined rather quickly by another ambiguous episode that shows Bevis to feel a little too comfortable in Ermin's Saracen world. As Calkin emphasizes, the text's anxiety about Christians living in the Saracen world "going native" reaches its climax when Bevis, now a knight at Ermin's court, meets his cousin Terri while travelling to Damascus to deliver a message to the Saracen king Brademond.[70] Instead of joyfully embracing his cousin, Bevis lies to Terri, telling him that he just saw Bevis hanged by the Saracens.[71] Here, Bevis goes a step further in enjoying his ability to pass. On the occasion of the Christmas Day battle, he desperately wanted to differentiate himself from his Saracen companions. During his encounter with Terri, on the contrary, he severs all ties with his biological European family, presumably to forge deeper bonds with his adoptive Saracen kin—especially Ermin, whom he believes loves him as a brother.[72] Yet, according to Carole-Anne Tyler:

> The mark of passing successfully is the lack of a mark of passing, the lack of a signifier of some difference from what one seems to be. Passing, therefore, can only name the very failure of passing, an indication of a certain contradiction at its heart, an indication of the contradictions which constitute it.[73]

When Bevis succeeds in convincing Terri to cease searching for him, he has in effect erased any remaining difference between what he is and what he seems to be, thereby eliminating the last of what separated him from the Saracens, whose identity he has donned as a disguise. In order both to re-assert his Christianity and to signal precisely his talent at passing, Bevis must engage in an activity that will clearly and definitely distinguish him from the Saracens. It is, therefore, hardly surprising that, upon arriving in Damascus, Bevis immediately and for no apparent reason sets himself the task of running to the nearest mosque, killing its "priest," and desecrating the Saracen gods.[74] Clearly, Bevis's "model of Christian heroism...melds violence with distinctively non-Saracen behaviour."[75]

---

68 Bevis's Saracen acquaintances do not realize the extent of Bevis's transformation. Whereas Bevis alternates between losing sight of his European background and asserting his Christian identity violently, his Saracen companions consistently refer to him as Christian and expect him to act as a Christian knight would.

69 Helen Young goes further, arguing that Bevis's Christianity "is linked to his Englishness and the challenge to his religious identity is answered at the same time as the importance of his nationality is reinforced." Young, *Constructing "England,"* 148.

70 Calkin, "Anxieties of Encounter," 141–42.

71 *Bevis of Hampton*, lines 1305–8.

72 *Bevis of Hampton*, lines 1330–32.

73 Carole-Anne Tyler, "Passing: Narcissism, Identity, and Difference," *differences*, 6, no. 2–3 (Summer–Fall 1994): 215–16.

74 *Bevis of Hampton*, lines 1353–57.

75 Calkin, "Anxieties of Encounter," 143.

Bevis's violent affirmation of his Christian identity is, however, too little too late, and he quickly pays for his temporary renunciation of his Christian faith and family. After his summary execution of the Saracen religious man and his toppling of the idols at the mosque of Damascus, Bevis heads to Brademond's castle to deliver Ermin's message, only to discover that the letter he has carried all the way from Armenia calls for his own death. Brademond throws the hero into prison, binding him to a large stone and hurling him into a pit filled with snakes.[76] As Kenneth D. Eckert has argued, the presence of snakes—and more specifically adders—at the bottom of the pit is highly charged symbolically: Bevis revealed his affection for his Saracen lord when he told Terri that he was dead, and his struggle for his life against snakes mirrors his attempt to preserve his spiritual survival after making such a disastrous mistake.[77]

Once again, we might expect the hero's trajectory to resume along familiar, conventional lines: having lost sight of his true identity after his initial journey to the Saracen world, it would make sense for Bevis to grasp the superiority of his original, Christian identity. One could argue that the time has come for Bevis to embark on his return journey to Europe, one that would parallel his first, coerced one while signaling his growth into a mature character. Indeed, Bevis does appear to have learned the error of his "passing" days at this point in the text, and the activities in which he engages now cast him in a heroic Christian light. Upon his release from Brademond's prison, he kills a giant, visits the patriarch of Jerusalem, and later defeats and kills a dragon like a new St. George.

Despite these Christian deeds, Bevis chooses to remain in the Saracen world after regaining his freedom. When he makes this decision, he articulates why he will not use his newfound freedom and mobility to return to his native land:

> "Lord," a thoughte, "whar mai I gone?
> Whar ich in to Ingelonde fare?
> Nai," a thoughte, "what scholde I thare,
> Boute yif ichadde ost to gader,
>
> For to sle me stifader?"
> He thoughte, that he wolde an hie
> In to the londe of Ermonie,
> To Ermonie, that was is bane,
> To his lemman Josiane.[78]
>
> "Lord," he thought, "Where may I go?
> Where am I to go in England?
> No," he thought, "What should I do there,
> Unless I had an army assembled,
> To slay my stepfather?"

---

76 *Bevis of Hampton*, lines 1423–26.

77 Kenneth D. Eckert, "Bad Animals and Faithful Beasts in *Bevis of Hampton*," *Neophilologus*, 97, no. 3 (2013): 584–85. Bevis's struggle against fiendish snakes at the bottom of Brademond's pit also recalls Eve's temptation in the Garden of Eden. Like a new, improved Eve, Bevis strikes and kills the adders torturing him rather than giving in to them.

78 *Bevis of Hampton*, lines 1976–84.

> He thought that he would hurry on
> To the land of Armenia,
> To Armenia, that was his death,
> To his lover Josian.

Bevis's announcement that he will go to Armenia rather than England allows the narrator to revert our attention to Josian and her relationship with Bevis. Nevertheless, Bevis's immediate and categorical rejection of a possible return to England is striking. His release from Brademond's jail, following as it does his betrayal by an important member of his Saracen "family," provides the perfect occasion to turn to Hampton. His ties with the Saracen world now severed, he is free to pre-occupy himself solely with his European affairs. That he elects not to journey to England to re-appropriate his lands from the emperor of Germany indicates the depth of his bond with Ermin, Josian, and other Saracens. He almost seems to be looking for an excuse to stay in the Saracen world.

Moreover, Bevis presents England as a negative entity. Whereas the Saracen world embodies his hope for love and companionship, England is the site of war, death, and violence. In spite of all that has passed since Ermin's betrayal, Bevis still recognizes the Saracen world as a place of comfort and support, one that stands in contrast to an English homeland construed as brutal and destructive.[79]

Meanwhile, Josian waits for Bevis. Josian first states her intent to become a Christian early in the narrative, shortly after the Christmas Day Battle. However, the sincerity of that announcement is undermined by the fact that she has just called on "Mahoun."[80] When Bevis is treacherously held captive in Damascus, Josian shows her true feelings about Christianity, lamenting the falsehood of Bevis and his God. Throughout this period and, indeed, through her courtship of Bevis and her baptism, Josian shows no predilection for Christianity, a faith she adopts—as in the case of Becket's mother of legend—simply to marry the man she loves.

After her reunion with Bevis, Josian's resistance to her new religion becomes more restrained, linked as it is to her relationship with the Saracen giant Ascopard. In her

---

79 At this point, Bevis's understanding of his relationship to England and Armenia seems, at best, compromised. While his childhood experiences in England traumatized him, Ermin's betrayal led to his being imprisoned in a pit for seven years, an event whose significance is highlighted when the narrator calls Armenia Bevis's "bane" (*Bevis of Hampton*, line 1983). To the text's narrator and its audience, the Saracen world can no longer provide comfort to the hero at this point in the narrative. Yet, Bevis refuses to accept this truth: for him, Armenia and its neighbours remain full of promise. The light in which Bevis casts England on the one hand and the Saracen world on the other thus further reinforces that Bevis's journey East has profoundly affected him.

80 *Bevis of Hampton*, line 1118. Josian then declares her intent to convert to Christianity at lines 1194–96:

> "And ich wile right now to mede
> Min false godes al forsake
> And Cristendom for thee love take!"

> "And I will right now as a reward
> Forsake all my false gods
> And accept Christianity for your love!"

essay "Ascopard's Betrayal: A Narrative Problem," Melissa Furrow examines Ascopard's function in the text in light of his connection to Bevis.[81] Yet, I would argue that Ascopard is closest to Josian, this precisely because he personifies the Saracen world she has had to abandon. From the moment she first encounters Ascopard, Josian does everything she can to keep him by her side. She pleads with Bevis to let him live when her lover defeats the giant in combat. Later, when Bevis leaves Cologne to settle his dispute with his stepfather, Josian insists on Ascopard remaining with her. The exchange between the two lovers is especially telling:

> Beves sede "Lemman min,
> Min em, the Bischop Florentin,
> And Ascopard, me gode page,
> Schel thee warde fro damage."
> "Ye, have ich Ascopard," she sede,
> Of no man ne stant me drede;
> Ich take thee God and seinte Marie:
> Sone so thow might, to me thow highe!"

> Bevis said "My darling,
> My uncle, Bishop Florentin
> And Ascopard, my good page,
> Shall protect you from harm."
> "Yes, as long as I have Ascopard," she said,
> "I dread no man;
> I put you in the hands of God and Holy Mary:
> As soon as you can, return to me!"[82]

In asserting her reliance on Ascopard, Josian ignores the first half of Bevis's statement, namely that his uncle, the bishop Saber Florentin, will watch over her. Josian's own words are likewise significant: she places Bevis under the protection of God and the Virgin, but favours the very physical and Saracen company of Ascopard herself. Her preference for Ascopard—over the bishop, the Virgin, and even God himself—suggests that Josian has not yet let go of the Saracen world. In this moment, Josian shows that her baptism has not fully transformed her into a Christian lady. When confronted with the temporary loss of Bevis, she takes refuge not in God or in a Christian friend or relative but in the one Saracen companion left her. I would argue that Ascopard here serves as a double to Josian; he represents the Saracen self she has had to shed in order to obtain Bevis's love.[83]

When Ascopard inevitably betrays Josian and captures her on behalf of her first, Saracen husband, King Yvor of Mombraunt, much later in the narrative, Josian has still not fully assimilated into Latin Christian society. Even though she has, by this point in

---

81 Melissa Furrow, "Ascopard's Betrayal: A Narrative Problem," in *Sir Bevis of Hampton in Literary Tradition*, ed. Jennifer Fellows and Ivana Djordjević (Cambridge: Brewer, 2008), 145–60.

82 *Bevis of Hampton*, lines 2943–50.

83 Ascopard fails Josian shortly after she makes this ambiguous statement. Although Ascopard does not deliberately betray Josian on this occasion, he is easily deceived into leaving her alone by Earl Miles. *Bevis of Hampton*, lines 3137–54.

the story, married Bevis and birthed twin boys, she resorts to knowledge acquired in Armenia when she gives herself the appearance of a leper to repel her Saracen lover, privileging knowledge acquired in the Saracen world of her birth to divine Christian assistance to navigate her new, perilous circumstances. In fact, her behaviour in this episode recalls that of another Saracen princess, the heroine of the thirteenth-century Old French *chantefable Aucassin et Nicolete*, whose own blackface performance allows her to identify "as both black and white, Christian and Muslim" while also playing with her gender and class.[84] As Siobhain Bly Calkin has argued in "The Anxieties of Encounter and Exchange: Saracens and Christian Heroism in *Sir Beves of Hamtoun*," "her use of such knowledge demonstrates her continuing links to her heritage."[85] Despite having converted to Christianity and married a Christian lord, Josian remains rooted in her Saracen customs and ways.[86]

At the same time, Josian gives several indications of embracing her new Christian faith. The birth of Josian's twins is particularly significant in displaying Josian's changing attitude towards Christianity. When she goes in labour, she and Bevis are in a forest; yet, she refuses Bevis's assistance in birthing their children, invoking her female modesty and finally requesting "and let me worthe and Oure Levedy!" (and let me and Our Lady be!).[87] This passage is interesting in several different ways. First, Josian's allusion to her female modesty, her "privité," recalls an earlier episode in the romance in which Josian is forcibly married to Earl Miles after being left with Ascopard in Cologne. On that occasion, she uses the idea of female modesty—and the very same term—to deceive Miles into staying with her alone so as to kill him, thereby retaining her virginity and her hope of marrying Bevis upon his return.[88]

Likewise, Josian's relationship to the Virgin has shifted significantly. As mentioned above, Josian's earlier preference for the tangible presence of Ascopard over the spiritual support of Mary prior to Bevis's departure from Cologne marks her as, at the very least, uncertain about her new Christian faith. By contrast, when Josian calls on the Virgin to help deliver her children, she appears completely sincere. Where her call on Mary in the earlier passage seemed part of an attempt to "pass" as a Christian woman, a clever performance meant to convince Bevis that her baptism had truly changed her beliefs just as her allusion to her "privité" in her exchange with Miles served to deceive him, Josian now refuses human aid and turns to the Virgin in this most desperate of situations.

Also telling is Josian's transformation when she finally feels free to cast off her repulsive disguise and to allow her natural beauty to return. Just as with the Sultan of Damascus in *The King of Tars*, Josian undergoes a transformation that reveals the completion of her spiritual journey from a false faith in the Saracen gods to acceptance of the truth

---

84 Robert S. Sturges, "Race, Sex, Slavery: Reading Fanon with *Aucassin et Nicolette*," *postmedieval*, 6, no. 1 (2015): 15–16.

85 Calkin, "Anxieties of Encounter," 145.

86 Jacqueline de Weever notes that Saracen women are often presented as healers because of their knowledge of herbs. De Weever, *Sheba's Daughters*, 32.

87 *Bevis of Hampton*, line 3634.

88 Josian uses the word "privité" in these two very different contexts at lines 3200 and 3630.

of Christianity. That she reverts to her natural state while doing so demonstrates the ambiguous place of heathen women, whose whiteness underscores their potential for conversion even prior to baptism, in the medieval imaginary.[89]

Eventually, Josian demonstrates not only the authenticity of her conversion, but also that she has fully integrated into her new Christian community. Josian's assimilation in the feudal framework of Christian society becomes apparent in a much later episode. At the end of the poem, Bevis hears that the English king Edgar has dispossessed his cousin of his ancestral lands. A formidable battle ensues in the streets of London, and a rumor spreads that Bevis has died. When this false report reaches Josian, she enjoins their twin sons, Guy and Miles, to avenge their father's death.[90] In response, Guy and Miles fall on their knees and ask for their mother's blessing. The young men treat Josian as a powerful woman worthy of respect. Josian gives them a task, and they immediately obey her, paying homage to her prior to their departure. Through her sons, Josian is symbolically shown to possess an important place in her adoptive Christian community.

At this climactic moment, it is important to note not only what Josian does, namely using her voice to counsel her nearest male kin to take appropriate action, but also what she does not do. Unlike the earlier episode in which Ascopard betrays and kidnaps her, she does not resort to magic and lore acquired in the Saracen world. Even more significant is the fact that she does not take any action herself but rather demands her sons do so on the family's behalf. For these reasons, I would argue that this episode illustrates that, in time, Josian becomes a proper Christian lady. In Josian's case, assimilation does eventually follow upon conversion, but it takes years, decades even, for Josian's intent to convert to Christianity—first stated in Armenia very early in the poem—to lead to Josian's transformation from a Saracen princess into a Christian lady.

Yet, even when Josian shows herself to have truly embraced Christianity and assimilated into her new Christian community, we are reminded of her non-Christian, Eastern origins. When Josian is absconded by Ascopard after calling on the Virgin and revealing her growing belief in her new faith, Bevis refers to the twin boys she has left behind as "hethen" (heathen).[91] When Josian enjoins her sons to avenge their father, Guy and Miles ride away on exotic riding beasts as if to remind the poem's audience of the non-Western provenance of Josian and, by extension, her children.[92] The narrative thus seems intent on reminding us of Josian's original Saracen identity at the same time that it displays her transformation into a Christian lady.

No matter how laborious and drawn-out, Josian's conversion journey *does* succeed, but such is not the case for Ascopard, whose uncommon baptism fails. Because of the intimacy Ascopard enjoys with Bevis and Josian, Bevis's uncle, Bishop Saber Florentin of

---

89 Jones-Wagner, "The Body of the Saracen Princess."
90 *Bevis of Hampton*, lines 4465–67.
91 *Bevis of Hampton*, lines 3714 and 3734.
92 Guy rides an Arabian horse while Miles is mounted on a camel. *Bevis of Hampton*, lines 4475 and 4481, respectively. Amy Burge likewise notes the mounts of Bevis's sons, stating that they reveal "their non-Englishness by riding into London to save their father on an Arabian horse and a camel." Burge, *Representing Difference*, 69.

Cologne, expects that Ascopard will convert alongside Josian. To accommodate the oversize Ascopard, the bishop has a special font prepared. At the crucial moment, however, Ascopard refuses baptism, exclaiming:

> "Prest, wiltow me drenche?
> The devel yeve thee helle pine,
> Icham to meche te be cristine!"[93]

> "Priest, will you drown me?
> The devil give you hell's pain,
> I am too large to be christened!"

That Ascopard rejects baptism is significant. First, it provides a brief moment of levity in between episodes packed with action, adventure, and nail-biting tension. Secondly, it prepares the narrative's audience for Ascopard's betrayal of his Christian friends and his return to the Saracen world. Most importantly, perhaps, the episode of Ascopard's failed baptism speaks to the inability of some Saracens to accept baptism.[94] Ascopard's failed conversion hints at a racialization of the Other and a narrowing of who can and cannot be allowed into the Christian fold.

If Ascopard's inability to accept baptism and Josian's continued Othering long after her conversion suggest that the Saracen characters of *Bevis of Hampton* are racialized, their Saracen identity essentialized so as to render their alterity permanent and indelible, the narrative otherwise resists any simplistic interpretation of its representation of Christian-Saracen relations. Where a modern reader might expect the Saracen world to serve as a tool to the hero, providing shelter, comfort, and support to Bevis until such time that he can claim his inheritance and return to his rightful place in England, as Lynn Ramey has shown to be the case in several late medieval French works, Bevis never fully returns to England.[95] On the contrary, when Bevis has finally succeeded in winning recognition and approval in his native land, he chooses to go "home" to the Saracen kingdom of Mombraunt.[96] In the end, then, Lomperis's categories of "home" and "not home" finally collapse in *Bevis of Hampton*. No longer simply "passing," Bevis acknowledges that his home lies in the East and not in England. Just as with Josian and Ascopard, the East entices and beckons Bevis, and he is forever changed by his experiences in the Saracen world.

---

93 *Bevis of Hampton*, lines 2594–96.

94 Like Ascopard, King Yvor will prove himself incapable of accepting the truth of Christianity, preferring to die at Bevis's hands rather than convert. In his case, King Yvor simply states that "Cristene wile ich never ben, / For min is wel the beter lawe!" (Christian will I never be / For mine is the better law). *Bevis of Hampton*, lines 4232–33.

95 Lynn Tarte Ramey, *Christian, Saracen and Genre in Medieval French Literature* (New York: Routledge, 2001).

96 *Bevis of Hampton*, lines 4570–79.

Conclusions

Although baptism always plays a pivotal, often climactic role in medieval works dealing with the Other, I would argue that the treatment of conversion in medieval literature evolves along specific lines from the High to the late Middle Ages. The four works discussed above, the *Chanson de Roland*, the *Prise d'Orange*, *The King of Tars*, and *Bevis of Hampton*, provide us with a palimpsest into a collective shift in medieval popular thinking about conversion. Where the two twelfth-century texts present conversion as an event—baptism—that radically transforms an individual, allowing for immediate assimilation into the convert's new Christian community, the two fourteenth-century narratives depict conversion as a socio-cultural process. Unlike baptism, this process—and, therefore, assimilation into the Latin Christian *communitas*—can take a long time to complete, as in the case of Josian, or, as with Ascopard, never be fulfilled.

As baptism and conversion are gradually dissociated from each other, baptism becoming merely one step amongst many on the path to assimilation into Christian society, the need to differentiate between Christians and Saracens gains in urgency. Where the *Chanson de Roland* presents its readers with a relative absence of difference, the three later texts emphasize the physical, linguistic, and cultural factors that divide one group from the other. Interestingly, physical characteristics, particularly skin colour, are ultimately displaced by linguistic and cultural attributes. While the principal visible point of difference between Christians and Saracens in the *Prise d'Orange* lies in the Saracens' black skin, *Bevis of Hampton* shows much more concern in the behaviour, habits, and customs of individual characters. Josian, for example, can only be perceived as a true Christian when she renounces the associations, practices, and knowledge she acquired in the Saracen world of her birth. The replacement of hermeneutic blackness by primarily social and cultural phenomena signals a new way of thinking about conversion. This substitution also means that conversion is a more threatening prospect: *we* can no longer tell whether someone can integrate the Christian family simply by looking at them. Likewise, the process of conversion is now of much longer duration—as can again be seen in the case of Josian in *Bevis of Hampton*.

This new approach to conversion as a socio-cultural process upon which the convert must expand time and effort illustrates a heightened anxiety about identity in late medieval England. To what extent can *anyone* convert to Christianity? Ascopard, for one, is "to meche" to receive baptism.[97] If conversion is unlikely or downright impossible for certain individuals, are whole communities to be barred from baptism? And the biggest questions of all: at what point does conversion begin and when does this long, drawn-out process end? Are all conversions successful or are some, like the princess of Tars's nominal conversion to the Saracen faith, insincere?

The Becket legend, composed around the middle of the thirteenth century, is situated exactly as this shift is developing, and the narrative reveals both a profound interest in the East and an acknowledgment that baptism alone cannot guarantee assimilation into Christian society. In the next chapter, I turn to this relatively unfamiliar text and its layered approach to conversion.

---

97 *Bevis of Hampton*, line 2594.

Chapter 2

THOMAS BECKET'S MOTHER

In his biography of Thomas Becket, Frank Barlow dismisses the saint's parents, arguing that: "the remembered origins of the family were relatively humble."[1] The main histories chronicling Thomas's life do indeed describe Gilbert Becket and his wife as London burghers, who, though relatively comfortable, were distinguished neither by their birth nor by any extraordinary accomplishments. The most that can be said about Thomas's mother in these accounts is that she was a virtuous, zealous lady of Norman blood.

Within a hundred years of Thomas's martyrdom in Canterbury Cathedral, a very different version of the saint's parentage and birth had risen to prominence in popular lives of the saint. According to this new narrative, Gilbert had met a non-Christian princess while on pilgrimage, and his union to her led to the conception of Thomas on their wedding night. In fact, the fantastical narrative about Gilbert and the foreign princess soon came to dominate the early part of Thomas's lives and was presented as fact from the thirteenth to the twentieth centuries.

There exists three main versions of this legend. The earliest account to feature the narrative about Thomas Becket's non-Christian mother is the thirteenth-century *Later Quadrilogus* or *Quadrilogus I*.[2] Aside from several other pieces repeating the *Quadrilogus* narrative, two other versions of the legend appear by the end of the Middle Ages. The first of these, the thirteenth-century compilation of hagiographical narratives known collectively as *The South English Legendary*, might only postdate the *Quadrilogus* account by a few decades. The second, a Middle English translation of the *Legenda Aurea* or *Golden Legend* of Jacob of Voragine does not emerge until the early fifteenth century.

This chapter will focus on these three main versions of the Becket legend in order to provide the necessary information to this now relatively obscure text prior to exploring the treatment of conversion in the legend. The discussion of the Becket legend both returns us to the questions about conversion addressed in chapter one while also introducing the main aspects of the legend as a preliminary to an exploration of its intersection with Chaucer's *Man of Law's Tale* in subsequent chapters.

Becket's Mother in the Historical Accounts of His Life

Not much is said about Thomas Becket's parents in the biographies of Thomas composed by his contemporaries. In *The Lives of Thomas Becket*, Michael Staunton identifies thirteen accounts as the primary historical narratives of Thomas's life—those of Edward Grim, John of Salisbury, Benedict of Peterborough, William of Canterbury, William Fitzstephen, Guernes of Pont-Sainte-Maxence, Alan of Tewkesbury, and Herbert

---

[1] Frank Barlow, *Thomas Becket* (Berkeley: University of California Press, 1986), 11.
[2] Paul Alonzo Brown, *The Development of the Legend of Thomas Becket* (Philadelphia: University of Pennsylvania Press, 1930), 28n1.

of Bosham as well as the anonymous texts known as Anonymous I, Anonymous II, Anonymous III, the *Summa Causae inter regem et Thomam*, and the late fourteenth-century Icelandic *Thómas saga Erkibyskups*.[3] Although nine of these pieces were composed less than ten years after the archbishop's murder at the hands of four of Henry II's knights in Canterbury Cathedral, only John Salisbury, Edward Grim, William Fitzstephen, and the authors of *Anonymous I* and *Anonymous II* mention his parents and birth.[4] Of the later works, the account of Herbert of Bosham, completed between 1184 and 1186, and the Icelandic *Saga* also open by providing some information about Thomas's parents.[5] A few other, more minor accounts likewise briefly refer to Thomas's father and mother.

Those hagiographical accounts that do begin with a brief passage on Thomas's parents almost unanimously depict the Beckets as good, but non-noble residents of London. While many accounts—for example the work of Edward Grim—simply pass over the information that Thomas's parents were honest merchants and burghers, some emphasize the inferior status of his relations the better to reinforce Thomas's greatness. John of Salisbury's *vita* of Thomas, for instance, describes the saint as being "parentum mediocrium proles illustris / the illustrious offspring of inferior parents."

As stated succinctly by Robert Mills, Thomas's mother is described in the lives roughly contemporary with the saint's death as an English noblewoman named Matilda of Caen.[6] In fact, the picture of Thomas's mother that emerges in these early lives is rather more complicated. Although she is presented in all accounts as a Norman woman whose family hailed from France, her name is not always Matilda (or Mahalt). Of those texts that do provide a name for Thomas's mother, the work known as *Anonymous II* identifies her as Roesa rather than Matilda.[7] The two narratives that distinguish her the most clearly from her husband—*Anonymous I* and *Anonymous II*—stress her virtuous behaviour and conduct in great detail, presenting her as a model Christian woman prior to the conception and birth of her son. Of far greater interest to the authors of these lives, and presumably to their target audiences, are the dreams and visions imputed to the saint's mother after becoming pregnant, ones described in detail not only in *Anonymous I* and *II*, but also in the accounts of Edward Grim and Guernes of Pont-Sainte-Maxence.

Although the historical sources for Thomas Becket's life thus present his mother as Anglo-Norman, they are not overly concerned with her background and heritage. The

---

3 Michael Staunton, *The Lives of Thomas Becket* (Manchester: Manchester University Press, 2001), 6–11. In his own, slightly more extensive discussion of Thomas's hagiographers, Frank Barlow adds the names of Robert of Cricklade, whose influential early life of Thomas was lost, Benet of St. Albans, author of a later life in French, and the anonymous *Quadrilogus II*, which served as the basis for the *Quadrilogus I*. Barlow, *Thomas Becket*, 6–8.

4 Staunton, *Lives of Thomas Becket*, 7–9.

5 Staunton, *Lives of Thomas Becket*, 10–11.

6 Robert Mills, "The Early *South English Legendary* and Difference: Race, Place, Language, and Belief," in *The Texts and Contexts of Oxford, Bodleian Library, MS Laud Misc. 108: The Shaping of English Vernacular Narrative*, ed. Kimberly K. Bell and Julie Nelson Couch (Leiden: Brill, 2011), 209.

7 It is interesting to note that this account is also the one that refers to her coming from Caen in France, further complicating Mills's statement that the name of Thomas's historical mother was Matilda of Caen. Mills, "The Early *South English Legendary* and Difference," 209.

Table 1: Information about Thomas Becket's mother in historical accounts that provide some details about his parents.

	Anonymous I	Anonymous II	Herbert of Bosham	Edward Grim	William Fitzstephen	Thómas saga Erkibyskups	Guernes de Pont-Sainte-Maxence
Name	Matilda	Roesa	Matilda	Matilda	Mahalt	Maild	Mahalt
Family	From a good family	"from a family of burghers" similar to that of her husband	N/A	"by no means inferior to others"	N/A	"of good kin"	"de nette gent"
Area of family's origin	N/A	Caen	N/A	N/A	N/A	N/A	N/A
Virtue and piety	Known for her virtue, constancy, piety, devotion, and alms-giving	"Becoming in conduct" and "faithfully subjected by her own fear to God"	N/A	Upright, innocent, and pious	N/A	"rightwise before God"	N/A
Beauty	N/A	"beautiful in the arrangement of her body"	N/A	N/A	N/A	N/A	N/A
Visions	Yes	Yes	N/A	Yes	N/A	Yes	Yes

sources that do place more emphasis on Thomas's mother do so *after* the conception of the saint, when she is pregnant and given visions presaging her unborn son's greatness. The relative indifference for Thomas's mother found in these historical sources is drastically revised in the fantastical legend ascribed to the saint and his parents in later versions of his life.

The *Later Quadrilogus* and Related Accounts

One of the earliest accounts to feature the narrative about Thomas Becket's non-Christian mother is the work known as The *Later Quadrilogus* or *Quadrilogus I*. Based on *Quadrilogus II*, a historical account of Becket's life produced in the twelfth century and identified by prominent Becket biographers as one of the primary early sources dealing with the saint, The *Later Quadrilogus* has been preserved in two thirteenth-century manuscripts prior to its first printing in 1495.[8] It is very much possible that this version of the legend about Thomas Becket's foreign mother lies closest to the first iteration of the narrative.

The *Later Quadrilogus* is essential to understanding the development of St. Thomas's parentage not only because of its probable early date, but also because it identifies the main components of the legend. Gilbert Becket is a Londoner who leaves his native England to go on pilgrimage to the Holy Land. While visiting some holy sites, he is captured by a pagan prince. His new master takes a liking to Gilbert, inviting him to dine with him every night. Such repeated encounters with Gilbert lead the prince's daughter to seek him out, and she promises that she will convert to Christianity if he marries her. Gilbert hesitates to give his oath to his heathen lover and eventually escapes his prison alone. Upon discovering that the object of her desire has fled, the princess embarks on her own journey to London. Although her journey is initially rendered easier by travelling companions who speak her language, it becomes much more difficult for her to communicate when she reaches England because she knows no English and can only utter the word "London." Her situation hardly improves in London, where boys make fun of her strange language and clothing. Her suffering ends when she is recognized by Richard, Gilbert's servant who had followed him to the East and been captured alongside him. Not knowing what to do, Gilbert has her led to a neighbouring widow's house before turning to six bishops who just happen to be meeting at St. Paul's Cathedral at that very moment. The bishops decide that the princess has been divinely appointed to marry Gilbert, provided she accept baptism. A quick baptism and wedding ensue, and the couple conceives St. Thomas. Gilbert then wants to return to the Holy Land to complete his pilgrimage but feels he must remain in England to support his wife, who still cannot speak English. However, the newly baptized princess enjoins her husband to pursue his dream, assuring him that all will be well in his absence. Gilbert leaves England for three and a half years, then returns to Thomas, now "a beautiful child, and held in high esteem in the eyes of all."[9] Her

---

[8] Brown, *The Development of the Legend of Thomas Becket*, 28n1.
[9] Brown, *The Development of the Legend of Thomas Becket*, 32.

mission of bringing her saintly son into the world now accomplished, the princess vanishes from Thomas's life.

Paul Alonzo Brown identifies four different sets of texts as nearly identical to the narrative found in The *Later Quadrilogus*: the account of the legend in the manuscripts Harley 978—dated to about 1260–1270—and Cotton Julius D6, the fifteenth-century chronicle attributed to John Brompton in Roger Twysden's *Decem scriptores* (1652), and some versions of the life of Thomas Becket by Edward Grim.[10] Most texts replicate the *Quadrilogus* narrative almost verbatim, for example the versions of Grim's life that include the legend about Thomas's foreign mother and the piece by Brompton.[11] The opening paragraph of John Brompton's treatment of the legend, however, sets this version of the legend apart from others. In his introduction to the legend, Brompton identifies Thomas's mother as Matilda, repeating almost verbatim the information provided by Edward Grim on Thomas's historical mother. After this historical opening, Brompton reiterates the narrative given in The *Later Quadrilogus*, MS. Cotton Julius D6, and certain versions of Edward Grim's work. Brompton's account thus provides an interesting blending of the historical and the legendary in dealing with Thomas's mother.[12]

One last work belongs to this group of texts, a version of the legend found in the *Vita Beati Thomae Martyris* by John Grandisone, bishop of Exeter from 1327 to 1369.[13] Although reduced to a third of the length of The *Later Quadrilogus* narrative and other fuller manifestations of the legend, Grandisone's account still describes the same story, albeit with much less detail and omitting the epilogue that reunites Gilbert with his son three and a half years after his departure from England to complete his pilgrimage. In the words of Paul Alonzo Brown, the account is "in substance the same as the *Quadrilogus* but considerably condensed."[14]

---

[10] Brown, *The Development of the Legend of Thomas Becket*, 28.

[11] Brown, *The Development of the Legend of Thomas Becket*, 28n2 and 28n3.

[12] The account of Thomas's legend attributed to Laurentius Wade and dated to 1497 replicates this mixture of historical and legendary when dealing with Thomas's Saracen mother. Brown, *The Development of the Legend of Thomas Becket*, 36. While this late medieval version of the narrative— in Middle English with Latin headings—offers another reiteration of the legend ascribing a non-Christian mother to Thomas Becket, it begins by introducing the princess as the daughter of Gilbert's Saracen captor. The Saracen prince, named Admyralde, has a daughter "fulle fayr wnto syghte, / [and] Whos name was Mawde" (very fair to see / Whose name was Maud). Wade refers to John (Grandisone), Bishop of Exeter as his source for his treatment of the legend about Thomas Becket's Saracen mother. C. Horstmann, ed., "Thomas Beket, Epische Legende, von Laurentius Wade (1497)," *Englische Studien* III (1880): 409–69 at 412.

[13] Brown, *The Development of the Legend of Thomas Becket*, 34. Another shortened version of the legend can be found in *Mirk's Festial*. Much briefer than Grandisone's treatment of the story, the account in *Mirk's Festial* has been dated to the first quarter of the fifteenth century. In this very brief and much later version of the legend, Thomas's mother is simply "a worschypfull woman of the contrey" (an honourable woman from that country). Brown, *The Development of the Legend of Thomas Becket*, 35.

[14] Brown, *The Development of the Legend of Thomas Becket*, 34. An important alteration to the *Quadrilogus* narrative found in John Grandison's *Life of St. Thomas* is that, in this account, Gilbert Becket and his companion are "a sarazenis simul capti" (they were captured by the Saracens

Overall these various versions of the story are drawn from outside the traditional bounds of hagiography. Thomas's future mother acts very much the part of the Saracen princess of romance and *chanson de geste*.[15] She woos and pursues Gilbert while he remains entirely at the mercy of her father (and, therefore, herself), a standard staple of texts featuring Saracen princesses. Like scores of other Christian objects of desire of non-Christian women, Gilbert not only appears passive and vulnerable early on in the passage, but he also reacts to the princess's overtures with fear and suspicion rather than pleasure.

However, it is important to note that the princess is not identified as Saracen in The *Later Quadrilogus* and in other versions of the legend influenced by this work. Although it might be argued that the term "pagan" here *does* refer to inhabitants of the Muslim world, the author(s)' linguistic choice at the very least highlights that it does not particularly matter whence Thomas Becket's mother hails. What matters in The *Later Quadrilogus* and related texts is that Thomas's mother is not Christian and that Gilbert meets her while on pilgrimage to the Holy Land. Her pagan religion, indeterminate and uninteresting in and of itself, does not diminish the woman's value.

Also unlike the typical Saracen princess of romance and *chanson de geste*, Gilbert's lover is curiously lacking in aggression as she embarks upon her journey to England. Whereas many iterations of the Saracen princess motif prove their new allegiance by, at the very least, abetting in the killing of their Saracen relatives, Thomas's mother simply leaves her family. Any risk she encounters is to herself and not to others. Finally, and perhaps more importantly, the foreign princess has no material dowry to bestow upon Gilbert at their wedding. While Saracen princesses usually remain on Saracen territory, Gilbert's union leads to no territorial acquisition or massive conversion to Christianity. Thomas's mother is a foreign woman whose significance lies in her body and journey alone.

Gilbert's bride remains vulnerable even after her conversion. She still cannot speak English, leading Gilbert to express reticence at the idea of returning to the Holy Land for a second pilgrimage. If the princess still cannot function in English society on her own, she nevertheless manifests a new kind of agency as a Christian noblewoman and the mother of a future saint. Having gained a voice, the princess reveals her humanity and her potential for assimilation into Latin Christian society.

These different accounts, most of them quite detailed, lay the groundwork for further developments of the legend about Thomas Becket's mother. In the next few pages, I will examine several versions of the legend written in Middle English, ones that do not alter the narrative found in The *Later Quadrilogus* and related pieces in any substantial way but that add some interesting details and points of emphasis to the story of Gilbert Becket and his foreign bride.

---

together), thereby transforming the generic pagan Other into Saracens. Brown, *The Development of the Legend of Thomas Becket*, 269.

15 Sarah Kay convincingly argues that Saracen princesses belong in *chansons de geste* just as much as they do in romances and that to say otherwise reveals a desire to restrict our understanding of the *chansons* to that which reinforces our vision of them as purely male-centred, patriarchal works. Sarah Kay, *The Chansons de geste in the Age of Romance: Political Fictions* (Oxford: Clarendon, 1995), 30–48.

The South English Legendary

The thirteenth-century compilation of hagiographical narratives known collectively as *The South English Legendary* provides just such an example of a text that, while retracing the same story as the accounts described above, places more emphasis on certain details than others, thereby leading to the creation of a narrative that conveys a very different message from its Latin counterparts. Perhaps the greatest alteration made by the authors of *The South English Legendary* lies in its focus on Thomas's mother, subtly privileging her perspective and significance in Thomas's conception over that of the London-born Gilbert.

The South English Legendary first came to be designated as such by Carl Horstmann when he edited the text's earliest surviving manuscript in 1887.[16] Since then, several scholars—starting with Thomas R. Liszka—have called for a slight modification to this title, arguing that the label *The South English Legendaries* better reflects the existence of multiple versions of the work and testifies to its flexibility and adaptability.[17] In the case of the depiction of Thomas Becket's mother, such textual variation produces some interesting nuances.

The South English Legendary first appeared towards the end of the thirteenth century and remained highly popular in England until the fifteenth century, with the preservation of over sixty full manuscripts attesting to widespread interest in it.[18] The *SEL* offers a variety "of readings for the feasts of the Church," combining both *sanctorale*, that is saints' lives, and *temporale*, moveable feasts.[19] Perhaps because it was produced for a lay audience, the collection is "arranged not according to the church calendar, which begins with Advent, but according to the secular calendar, beginning 1 January."[20] Although the *SEL* is based in part on the famous *Legenda aurea* or *Golden Legend*, the English liturgical tradition probably played a far more important role than its more famous counterpart in shaping it.[21] The text is thoroughly English: composed in southern England, it derives from earlier English religious writings and is intended for a regional English audience.

---

16 Thomas R. Liszka, "The South English Legendaries," in *The North Sea World in the Middle Ages: Studies in the Cultural History of North-Western Europe*, ed. Thomas R. Liszka and Lorna E. M. Walker (Dublin: Four Courts, 2001), 243 and 245. Carl Hortsmann, ed. *The Early South-English Legendary; or, Lives of Saints. I. Ms. Laud 108, in the Bodleian Library*, Early English Text Society, o.s., 87 (London, 1887).

17 Liszka, "The South English Legendaries," 261.

18 Heather Blurton and Jocelyn Wogan-Browne, "Rethinking the *South English Legendaries*," in *Rethinking the South English Legendaries*, ed. Heather Blurton and Jocelyn Wogan-Browne (Manchester: Manchester University Press, 2011), 3.

19 Liszka, "The South English Legendaries," 244.

20 Liszka, "The South English Legendaries," 244. For more on the authorship, reception, and social context of thirteenth-century English vernacular works, see John Frankis, "The Social Context of Vernacular Writing in Thirteenth-Century England: The Evidence of the Manuscripts," in Blurton and Wogan-Browne, *Rethinking the South English Legendaries*, 66–83.

21 Sherry Reames, "*The South English Legendary* and Its Major Latin Models," in Blurton and Wogan-Browne, *Rethinking the South English Legendaries*, 84–85.

CHAPTER 2

Several manuscripts of this complex work have survived. The earliest known manuscript of *The South English Legendary*, Bodleian Library MS Laud Miscellaneous 108 (L), dates to about 1280.[22] Two other important early manuscripts of the *SEL* are Corpus Christi College Cambridge MS 145 (C) and British Library MS Harley 2277 (H), the latter only postdating the Laud manuscript (L) by about twenty years.[23] In addition to these three early manuscripts, I will also discuss briefly a late fifteenth-century manuscript that re-shapes the non-Christian identity of Thomas Becket's legendary mother in some intriguing ways.

As Robert Mills has argued, "the transfer of the Becket story from one *South English Legendary* collection to another produces a certain amount of variation," and one such area of deviation lies in the identity and treatment of Thomas Becket's mother.[24] In L, the importance of Thomas's mother is emphasized from the onset:

> Wolle ye nouthe i-heore this englische tale : that is here i-write
> Of seint Thomas of Caunterburi : al-hou he was bi-yite?
> Of londone is fader was : A bordeys hende and fre,
> Gilbert Bekat was is name : the bok tellez me.
> Ake is Moder was of hethenesse. : nov sone ye mouwen i-heore
> Al-hou heo cam into engelonde : are heo i-cristned were.[25]

> You will now hear this English tale that is here written
> Of Saint Thomas of Canterbury, how he was begotten
> His father came from London, a burgher courteous and noble,
> Gilbert Becket was his name; the book tells me.
> And his mother came from heathendom, now soon you shall hear
> How she came to England and how she was christened.[26]

According to this version, the Saracen princess shares the spotlight with Gilbert Becket, and it is suggested that she played a part just as essential—if not more so—than her Christian husband in conceiving their saintly son. As in The *Later Quadrilogus*, Thomas's foreign mother is introduced as a native of "hethenesse" and not necessarily a Saracen. Furthermore, the narrative makes it clear that this is the story of both Thomas's "fader" and his "moder," Gilbert's native "londone" paralleled with the "hethenesse" from which his bride hails at lines three and five, respectively, of the opening to the legend.

---

22 Liszka, "The South English Legendaries," 243 and 245. Carl Horstmann's edition of the work, *The Early South-English Legendary or Lives of Saints*, is based on the Laud manuscript.

23 Liszka, "The South English Legendaries," 243. Charlotte D'Evelyn and Anna J. Mill based their own edition of the *SEL* on these two slightly later manuscripts. Their edition of the Becket legend and the subsequent life of Becket is transcribed primarily from Corpus Christi College Cambridge MS 145 (C) with notes referring to alternate language and spelling in H as well as Bodley MS Ashmole 43 and British Museum MS Cotton Julius D. IX. Charlotte D'Evelyn and Anna J. Mill, ed. *The South English Legendary*, Early English Text Society, o.s., 236 (London, 1956–59).

24 Robert Mills, "Invisible Translation, Language Difference and the Scandal of Becket's Mother," in *Rethinking Medieval Translation: Ethics, Politics, Theory*, ed. Emma Campbell and Robert Mills (Cambridge: Brewer, 2012), 137.

25 *The Early South-English Legendary*, lines 1–6.

26 All translations in this chapter are my own.

Thomas's mother is identified in three different ways throughout L. Although not named until her baptism in London, the princess is initially defined by her relationship to her father, and she is referred to in the first part of the narrative as the amiral's daughter. In the second part of this version, one where her character inhabits a liminal space in more ways than one—she is on the sea, in between lands, religions, and identities—she becomes simply "heo" / "she." After her arrival in England, baptism, and marriage to Gilbert, she is labeled by her new Christian name, Alisaundre.[27]

As in The *Later Quadrilogus* and related accounts, the princess's non-Christian status is thus both significant and not. On the one hand, it is still important for Thomas's mother to possess Eastern roots and for Gilbert to meet her while on his way to the Holy Land. At the same time, the princess's religion of origin is not in itself important, and the narrative necessitates no more than a blanket reference to her "heathenness." Her encounter with Gilbert must be deemed miraculous, an act of God directed towards a virtuous, pious Englishman and one that will lead to the birth of the great English saint Thomas, but the religious community to which she belongs prior to her encounter with her father's Christian captive occasions little to no interest.

Thomas's mother in L is also presented as very strong, and her pursuit of Gilbert Becket is aggressive and almost threatening. During her first private exchange with Gilbert, she peppers him with questions about his religion. But her love for her father's Christian prisoner does not become visible until much later in the narrative. The amiral's daughter keeps her counsel to herself, and Gilbert's fear that she will betray him seems understandable.

By contrast, in C and H, only Gilbert Becket merits a reference at the beginning of the narrative, and his *Saracen* bride-to-be is not introduced until Gilbert has gone to the Holy Land and become her father's slave:

Gilberd was sein Thomas fader	that triwe man was & god
He louede God & Holy Churche	suththe he wit vnderstod
The crois to the Holy Lond	inis yonghede he nom
And mid on Richard that was is man	to Ierusalem he com
So that amang Sarazins	hi were inome attelaste
Hi and othere Cristenemen	and in strang prison ido
In miseise & in pine inou	in honger & chile also
In strang swinch night & day	to of swinke hore me[te] stronge[28]
Gilbert was Saint Thomas's father	he was an honorable and good man
He loved God and the Holy Church	since he reached the age of reason
The cross to the Holy Land	he took in his youth

---

27 *The Early South-English Legendary*, line 141. In the words of Robert Mills, the princess's new name "enables her finally to assume a place within the Christian community...the choice of name itself is potentially significant in linking the daughter with an identifiable location: baptism gives her a clear place in the world." Robert Mills, "Conversion, Translation and Becket's 'heathen' Mother," in Blurton and Wogan-Browne, *Rethinking the South English Legendaries*, 389. However, it must also be noted that the princess is primarily referred to as Gilbert's wife at the end of L.

28 *The South English Legendary*, lines 1–10.

CHAPTER 2

> And with Richard that was   his servant he came to Jerusalem
> So that among Saracens   they were taken at last
> They and other Christian men   and in a foreign prison thrown
> In much misery and torment   in hunger and cold also
> In hard toil night and day   to labor with difficulty for their food

Where L introduces its audience to both Gilbert Becket and the foreign princess who will become his bride, C and H focus only on Gilbert. In fact, the lines highlighting the heathen princess are replaced in the later manuscripts by a detailed discussion of Gilbert's piety and his first pilgrimage to Jerusalem. Thomas's mother is only introduced after her father has captured Gilbert:

> And ofte the prince also god in conseil him wolde drawe
> And the manere of Engelond   him esste and of the lawe
> So that me wolde is felawes muche god ofte do
> For is loue & alle hi uerde the bet for him also
> And nameliche for a maide that louede this Gilberd uaste
> The princes doghter Amiraud   that hure heorte al upe him caste
> And louede him in triwe loue   in gret mornynge and wo[29]

> And often the prince would draw him in counsel
> And asked him about the customs and the law of England
> So that he would often do his fellows much good
> For his love and they all fared the better for him also
> And namely for a maid that loved this Gilbert greatly
> The prince's daughter, Amiraud, that cast her heart upon him
> And loved him with true love in great mourning and woe.

Once introduced into the narrative, Thomas Becket's mother is defined by her love for Gilbert Becket in C and H. In fact, she is at first simply "a maide that lovede this Gilberd uaste," this even before her name, "Amiraud," is given.[30] Because the princess is sentimentalized in this way, the questions she poses Gilbert cannot be perceived as threatening in this version of the legend. This iteration of Becket's non-Christian mother is thus more positive but also less powerful than the character found in L. Like most Saracen princesses of romances and *chansons de geste*, the princess is simply a woman driven to conversion to Christianity and love of God by romantic love for a Christian man.

With the exception of the princess's baptismal name in L, the three manuscripts, L, C, and H, display more uniformity in their depiction of Thomas's mother in the second part of the narrative. Unlike the Latin versions of the legend, the author(s) of *The South English Legendary* underscores that the journey of the Saracen princess is no ordinary one, but rather ordained and guided by God himself. Where the Latin texts provide realistic details that explain how a woman who knows nothing of England might successfully reach London—for example, by providing her with fellow travellers who can translate

---

[29] *The South English Legendary*, lines 1–23. The only difference between C and H in this passage occurs at line 23: in H, the princess's love is described as "durne" rather than "triwe."

[30] *The South English Legendary*, line 21. George Alonzo Brown notes that the princess is given a name prior to baptism in MS. Ashmole 43. Brown, *The Development of the Legend of Thomas Becket*, 33.

and interpret English for her—the *SEL* narrative highlights that the journey was only possible through the will of God. The versions of the account in L, C, and H strongly suggest that her determination should not be regarded as an expression of her free will; instead God's will inspires and drives her to seek London and Gilbert despite her ignorance and fears.[31] This shift is especially potent in L, in which the Saracen princess is transformed from an independent agent into a vehicle of God's will in a matter of a few lines.[32] At this point, Becket's mother has come to embody some of the traits more typically associated with hagiography: she foregoes her own agency and free will in order to allow God to act through her.

Once in England, the Saracen princess of the *SEL* narrative undergoes yet another transformation as she steps into the genre of "wonder" literature and becomes a "marvel" to the Londoners she encounters. Because she can do nothing more than make strange, unintelligible noises, she has to endure the looks and derision of young and old alike. The language used to describe her at this critical juncture depicts her as somehow less than fully human: she is "ase a best" (like a beast) and "wonderful" (marvellous) in L and "as a best that ne couthe no wisdom / As he[o] were of another world" (like a beast lacking in intelligence / as if she were from another world), "a such mopiss best," (such a stupid beast), and a "wonder" (marvel) in C and H.[33]

All three manuscripts also underscore the princess's strength and resolve upon arrival in England. Gilbert's future bride stands firm, stating that she will either marry her beloved or return to her own land, a powerful stance upon which both George Alonzo Brown and Shokoofeh Rajabzadeh have remarked.[34] Not only does the princess clearly delineate the terms of her baptism and permanent removal to England, but she continues to assert herself even after her marriage. When she finds out, immediately after the wedding and conception of Thomas, that Gilbert wants to return to the Holy Land to complete his pilgrimage, she insists that he go, provided he leave his servant with her. Because the man accompanied Gilbert on his first pilgrimage and was captured along with his master by the amiral, he knows her language and can act as an interpreter for her until she learns English, she explains. Again, Thomas's future mother is seen planning and negotiating the terms of her assimilation into English Christian society. According to Rajabzadeh:

> Rather than submit to English social norms, erase, and forget her language, she insists on maintaining a structure of translation in her domestic space that accommodates her difference. The knave, like Gilbert, not only provides her comfort in her domestic space, "hire solas beo," but he also makes it possible for her to maintain a connection with the English world beyond her home while maintaining part of her identity...She may be for-

---

31 *The Early South-English Legendary*, lines 54–56 and *The South English Legendary*, line 70.

32 Mills, "Conversion, Translation and Becket's 'heathen' Mother," 387.

33 *The Early South-English Legendary*, lines 65 and 68 and *The South English Legendary*, lines 76–78 and 80.

34 Brown, *The Development of the Legend of Thomas Becket*, 33; Shokoofeh Rajabzadeh, "Alisaundre Becket: Thomas's Resilient, Muslim, Arab Mother in the *South English Legendary*," *postmedieval*, 10, no. 3 (2019): 298.

eign and at a disadvantage, but if anything, she shows us over and over again that she is not a voiceless subaltern, resigned to being helpless, alone, and silent.[35]

Thomas's mother is thus presented as a tool of divine agency, but also as a strong, independent individual in her own right.

The version of the legend found in the *SEL* differs from that in The *Later Quadrilogus*, some lives of Edward Grim, and the chronicles of John Brompton and John Grandisone by the reappearance of Thomas's mother at the very end of the account. When Gilbert finally returns to England, the author notes that both Thomas and his wife are doing well. The princess has, by this point, fully assimilated into English society and become the kind of maternal presence recognizable as a stock figure of hagiographical narratives.

Finally, one last version of *The South English Legendary* deserves mention, a much later manuscript dating to the fifteenth century and referenced as MS. Rawlinson F. 225. Although containing some elements added to the legend later in its development, this manuscript combines aspects of L, C, and H, particularly in its treatment of Thomas's mother. The portrait of Thomas's non-Christian mother in this late manuscript initially recalls her introduction in L:

I wil to yow rede	hov seynt Thomas was begetin & born
In oure begynnyg tht kyng vs spede	tht bar the holy corvn of thorn
A riche burgees of lond & lede	Of lundon cite his fadir was born
Gilbert Beket wyse man in dede	his name is callyd thus aforn
Beforn yow alle more & lasse	to yow I say this storye
His modir was born in hednes	in the lond of Ivrie[36]
I will read to you	how Saint Thomas was begotten and born
In our beginning may that king	that bore the holy crown of thorns give us prosperity
A rich burgher of land and men	in London the city his father was born
Gilbert Becket, a wise man in deeds,	his name was
Before you all, noble and common	to you I tell this story
His mother was born in heathendom	in the land of Jewry

As was the case in L, the princess is introduced early in the preface to Thomas Becket's life, and she is described as coming from the land of "hednes" (heathendom). At the same time, other parts of the fifteenth-century manuscript narrative clearly bear the influence of corresponding passages in C and H:

Men wolden for his love only	to hys felawes good do
And so thei dedon the ievry for his love many mo	
And prinsepally tht mayden tht lovid gilbert faste	
The sovdon doughtter of Ivre	hir herte to hym caste
Sche louyd gilbert hertly in gret moornyng & woo[37]	

---

35 Rajabzadeh, "Alisaundre Becket," 299.

36 Brown, *The Development of the Legend of Thomas Becket*, 262, lines 5–10.

37 Brown, *The Development of the Legend of Thomas Becket*, 263, lines 43–47.

> Men would do good to his fellows for his love alone
> And so the Jewry did for his love many more [good deeds]
> And principally that maiden that loved Gilbert greatly
> The daughter of the Sultan of Jewry cast her heart upon him
> She loved Gilbert heartily in great mourning and woe

Just as in C and H, the princess is presented as being in love with Gilbert prior to her interview with him, and the focus on her feelings for her father's captive romanticizes her. In fact, the language used in lines 43 to 47 of the narrative echoes almost verbatim the passage at lines 17 to 23 in C and H, with the lines "that louede this Gilberd uaste" at line 21 of C and H becoming "tht lovid gilbert faste" at line 45 of Rawlinson F. 225, "that hure heorte al upe him caste" at line 22 of C and H becoming "hir herte to hym caste" at line 46 of the later manuscript, and again "in gret mornynge and wo" resonating with "in gret moornyng & woo" at line 47 of the Rawlinson manuscript.

In true romance fashion, the princess is named towards the end of the narrative, right after the dramatic climax of her baptism. The audience is then told that "thei turnyd hir hethen name anon / tht callid was first ysope & namyd hir ther Ione" (they changed her heathen name at once / she that was first called Ysope and they named her there Ione).[38] Just as romance heroines—for example, Enide in the twelfth-century poem *Erec et Enide* by Chrétien de Troyes—are named upon marriage to the hero, so is the princess given both her original and her new, Christian name at a crucial point of transition in her life. That she is given two names rather than one also melds the two earlier manuscript traditions, that of L, in which the princess is named upon baptism, and that of C and H, where Gilbert's future bride is named prior to her conversion.

The most intriguing aspect of this manifestation of the legend, however, is undoubtedly the princess's identification as a Jewish princess. Nor is this a point made in passing, but, rather, an element that is emphasized over and over again in this version of the narrative. Not only does the princess come from "hednes" in the Rawlinson manuscript, but she originates more specifically, from "hednes in the lond of Ivrie."[39] The word "Ivrie" is then repeated three times at lines 44, 46, and 120 and "iew" three more times at lines 75, 77, and 78. Further details also seem to be included primarily to remind the narrative's audience of the princess's original Jewish identity. For example, her private exchange with Gilbert takes place "on a sabbot day" (on a sabbath day).[40]

Why transform the fictional, non-Christian princess of Thomas Becket's origin story into a Jewish princess, one who still hails from the Middle East and who remains the daughter of a "sovdon," but who has metamorphosed from a generic pagan or a "Sarazin" into a Jewish princess? Robert Mills's answer to this question addresses the changing relationship between England and various non-Christian Others in the late medieval period:

> These modifications may simply reflect a desire to keep the narrative fashionably up-to-date: whichever group is in vogue as the enemy of the moment (or of the individuals

---

38 Brown, *The Development of the Legend of Thomas Becket*, 267, lines 197–98.

39 Brown, *The Development of the Legend of Thomas Becket*, 262, line 10.

40 Brown, *The Development of the Legend of Thomas Becket*, 263, line 36.

who commissioned the manuscript in question) becomes the target of the hagiographer's condescending gaze.[41]

Implicit to Robert Mills's argument is the belief that Thomas's legendary non-Christian mother must be associated with the Other and that the relationship between England and that Other must be hostile. Moreover, the identity of the marginalized group to which Thomas's mother belongs is constantly shifting, dependent on the place and time at which any given version of the legend is produced.

I agree with Robert Mills that the identity of Thomas's mother changes considerably over time; however, I would argue for a slightly different interpretation of the meaning of this shift. Where the legend always identifies Thomas Becket's mother as foreign, she is also always safely distant and removed from late medieval England. In L, she is a heathen, a generic term with connotations to the Muslim world but also to the Roman Empire, and, in C and H, she is a "Sarazin" and, therefore, part of a group treated to some degree as a fantastical marvel in medieval writings of Western Europe. Should we treat it as a coincidence, then, that Thomas's mother comes to be identified as Jewish in a fifteenth-century manuscript? At the time of the production of Rawlinson F. 225, Jewish Englishmen and women had been forced out of their homes for over a hundred years. In that time, they had, perhaps, attained a somewhat mythical and fabulous status of their own in the English imaginary. This late iteration of the Becket legend raises interesting questions both about the place of Jews in the medieval English imaginary after the Expulsion of 1290 and about the conflation of Muslims and Jews in this same period, ones which I hope to delve upon at greater length in my next project.

For the purposes of this current study, it is important only to note that, regardless of her faith at birth, Thomas Becket's mother of legend always appears exotic and marvellous. By contrast, his father, Gilbert Becket, is rooted in the local and familiar world of London. It is a version of the Becket legend that emphasizes that less exciting—but also less threatening—aspect of the saint's story that I discuss next.

The Middle English Translation of the *Legenda Aurea*

If the version of the legend about Thomas Becket's mother found in *The South English Legendary* focuses on the non-Christian princess and God's intervention in the conception of the saintly Thomas, the narrative in the Middle English translation of the *Legenda Aurea* highlights the setting of the saint's birthplace. At least one manuscript of the Middle English translation of Jacob of Voragine's thirteenth-century *Legenda Aurea* includes the story of Gilbert Becket and his bride, depicted as in C and H as the daughter of a *Saracen* prince. This early fifteenth-century manuscript, British Museum Add. MS 11565, presents a version of events highly similar to that provided in *The South English Legendary*.[42] There exist, however, at least two interesting differences between the ver-

---

41 Mills, "Invisible Translation," 137.

42 The similarities linking different versions of *The South English Legendary* with the fifteenth-century translation of the *Legenda Aurea* begs the question as to whether the earlier English devotional text inspired the addition of this narrative to the translation into Middle English of Jacob of Voragine's work.

sion of the story found in *The South English Legendary*—especially in earlier manuscripts—and that of the fifteenth-century translation of the *Legenda Aurea*: the prose rendition of Thomas's conception narrative and the emphasis placed on London as a setting for the reunion of the lovers and the conception of Thomas Becket.[43]

That this later version of Thomas's conception narrative is written in prose rather than verse is perhaps more indicative of its late date than of any particular developments in the cult of Thomas Becket. Just as authors of romance shift from using verse to prose in the fifteenth and sixteenth centuries, so does the anonymous translator of the *Legenda Aurea* choose to use prose for his retelling of Voragine's seminal treatise on Christian saints. In this way, the development of this specific aspect of the Becket legend simply follows the evolution of the genre of romance in general, an observation that reinforces the ties between romance and the cult of Becket.[44]

Less obvious, but also interesting, is a detail that distinguishes this version of the Becket legend from earlier instances of it—especially earlier manuscripts of *The South English Legendary*.[45] On two separate occasions, at the beginning of the account and in the middle of it, the anonymous translator emphasizes the connection between Thomas Becket and the Church of St. Thomas of Acre. At the beginning of the piece, the author takes the time to note that "Gylbert beket was seint Thomas of Caunturbury is fader and borne in the Cite of London where seint Thomas of akers chirche is nowe" (Gilbert Becket was the father of St. Thomas of Canterbury and he was born in the city of London, where St. Thomas of Acre's church is now).

The connection with the Church of St. Thomas of Acre is reiterated in the middle of the account, as Thomas's mother arrives in London:

> And so atte laste by the puruyaunce of oure lorde she come ouer see in to englonde and so forth to London and when she come ayenst the place where Gilbert Beket dwellid there seint Thomas of Akirs is nowe she stode ful there.[46]

> And so at last through the provision of our Lord, she came overseas to England and on to London, and when she came to the place where Gilbert Becket dwelled, there where Saint Thomas of Acre is now, she stood completely there.

Although the linkage between Thomas Becket and Thomas of Acre was made earlier, as early in fact as the version of the legend found in The *Later Quadrilogus*, its emphasis

---

[43] Caxton uses the anonymous Middle English translation of the *Legenda Aurea* for his own version of the story in his 1483 edition of *The Golden Legend*. Brown, *The Development of the Legend of Thomas Becket*, 36. However, Caxton's treatment of the legend does not focus on London in the same way as the anonymous fifteenth-century translator of Jacob de Voragine's work. William Caxton, *The Golden Legend or Lives of the Saints, as Englished by William Caxton* (London: Dent, 1928), 2:182–84.

[44] As with manuscripts C and H of *The South English Legendary* and John Grandisone's *Life of St. Thomas*, Gilbert Becket and his companions "were take prisoners of the sarasyns" (were taken prisoner by the Saracens), and Thomas's future mother is truly a Saracen princess. Brown, *The Development of the Legend of Thomas Becket*, 271.

[45] This detail is present in the fifteenth-century version of *The South English Legendary*, but not in the earlier manuscripts of the *SEL* discussed above.

[46] Brown, *The Development of the Legend of Thomas Becket*, 272.

and repetition here is noteworthy. Referring to the Church or Hospital of St. Thomas of Acre founded in 1227 in the parish of St. Mary Colechurch by the Knights of St. Thomas, the first of the two passages cited above can be read in at least two different ways.[47] Either the allusion to this edifice is needed to help the text's audience identify London, the city where the well-known headquarters of the Knights of St. Thomas is located, or the passage, on the contrary, provides a specific reference that will help establish the setting of the second half of the legend to an audience already familiar with the city.

The second reference to the building reinforces the latter interpretation. In the second passage to the Church of St. Thomas of Acre, the anonymous translator appears to use the building not so much to help his audience identify the city in which his story is set, but rather to give as precise a location to the events he describes as possible. The phrase "there seint Thomas of Akirs is nowe" appears redundant and unnecessary to the construction of the sentence describing the place to which Thomas's mother has come. Unlike the earlier passage, in which the allusion to the church served to qualify London, this later mention does not serve any essential grammatical function in the sentence. In fact, the location of the Saracen princess has already been qualified by the comment that this is "the place where Gilbert Beket dwellid." The inclusion of the phrase about the Church of St. Thomas of Acre does, however, make sense if we imagine a contemporary audience made up of Londoners intent upon knowing the precise part of London in which the story takes place. To an audience of London burghers, the allusion to a building still very much a part of the fabric of their everyday life would give the legend a sense of immediacy and relevance not to be found in a mere reference to Gilbert Becket's residence.

The brief allusion to the Church of St. Thomas of Acre thus serves two important functions: It renders the connection between Thomas Becket and London more vivid and realistic to an audience probably made up primarily of London burghers, and it also reinforces the link between the cult of Becket and the Latin East. The two brief references to the Church of St. Thomas of Acre distinguish the narrative about Thomas's mother from other generic saints' lives ascribing miracles and idealized behaviour to their subjects and give the account an air of plausibility. Fantastical as it might be to think that Thomas's mother was a foreign princess ignorant of the English language and customs, her arrival at a site known and familiar to the text's audience makes the story more realistic than that of other saints and martyrs. If Thomas's mother was "here," then she must have been real. Of course, such logic is fallacy at best, but using the tangible, material Hospital of the Knights of St. Thomas as a marker for two of the major events in the story—the birth of Gilbert Becket and his reunion with his future son's mother—creates a bond between the legend's London audience and the saint. On the one hand, the story appears more realistic, if only on the most superficial level, because of its very real, very familiar setting, and, on the other, the story and its recognizable setting further impress that Thomas belongs not just to Canterbury, but also to London. Just as the story can serve as proof that Thomas's mother was a non-Christian princess driven by

---

[47] Lawrence Warner, "Adventurous Custance: St. Thomas of Acre and Chaucer's *Man of Law's Tale*," in *Place, Space, and Landscape in Medieval Narrative*, ed. Laura L. Howes (Knoxville: University of Tennessee Press, 2007), 44.

God to the shores of England to conceive the great saint, so can it be used as a means to tie Thomas to London.

By emphasizing both Thomas's connection to London and the saint's ties to the East, the anonymous translator of the *Legenda Aurea* further hints at the saint's association with the crusading movement. Katherine Lee Hodges-Kluck has argued in *The Matter of Jerusalem: The Holy Land in Angevin Court Culture and Identity, c. 1154–1216* that "Becket…functioned as a focal point for drawing together the political, spiritual, and physical landscapes of England and the Holy Land."[48] To Hodges-Kluck, Becket was used to support Angevin need to establish the relatively new dynasty as an important political force through engagement in Jerusalem, this especially in the events leading up to and during the Third Crusade.[49] What the anonymous Middle English translation of the *Legenda Aurea* suggests, however, is that, by the fifteenth century, the power that the Angevins had accrued through England's association with the Third Crusade, one in which the English saint served as an important spiritual tool, had been re-directed to serve the cult of Becket itself.

Before trying to draw some conclusions about the narrative transforming Thomas Becket's Anglo-Norman mother into a non-Christian princess, I will briefly mention one last medieval illustration of the legend: the manuscript illuminations portraying the arrival of Becket's mother on English soil, her baptism, her marriage to Gilbert, and the birth of Thomas in the early fourteenth-century manuscript catalogued as London, British Library, Royal 2.B.VII and commonly referred to as the Queen Mary Psalter. Robert Mills analyzes this visual representation of the legend in "Invisible Translation, Language Difference and the Scandal of Becket's Mother."[50] He notes that in the first of these four images, the princess appears unable to see, a visual signifier of her non-Christian status.[51] The princess is also singled out by her headdress, which differs from that of Christian women, rendering her foreignness visible.[52]

The next image depicting Thomas's mother focuses on her baptism. This second illumination vividly illustrates the power of this sacred rite:

> Our view of the woman in the baptism scene contrasts dramatically with the miniature depicting her arrival: gone is the head scarf, and she is now shown full frontal, eyes wide open, as if to indicate the moral transformation that has ensued.[53]

As in the case of Bramimonde in the *Chanson de Roland*, Orable in the *Prise d'Orange*, and the sultan in *The King of Tars*, conversion has fully and completely erased the princess's alterity.[54]

---

[48] Katherine Lee Hodges-Kluck, "The Matter of Jerusalem: The Holy Land in Angevin Court Culture and Identity, c. 1154–1216" (PhD diss., University of Tennessee, 2015), 73.

[49] Kluck, "The Matter of Jerusalem," 2.

[50] Mills, "Invisible Translation," 140.

[51] Mills, "Invisible Translation," 140.

[52] Mills, "Invisible Translation," 140.

[53] Mills, "Invisible Translation," 140.

[54] Mills, "Invisible Translation," 141.

The last two images depicting Thomas Becket's foreign mother in the Queen Mary Psalter further emphasize the absence of any essential difference in Becket's mother: In these last two miniatures, the newly converted princess is shown marrying Gilbert Becket and giving birth to Thomas. Altogether, the Queen Mary Psalter images stress the princess's initial difference only to highlight the power of conversion when Thomas's mother gains acceptance into Latin Christian English society following her baptism. This final manifestation of the legend thus shares one important commonality with the Middle English translation of the *Legenda Aurea*: both texts present an opposition between the local and the foreign, Gilbert's London and the princess's non-Christian, Eastern world. In the Queen Mary Psalter illuminations, however, the local and the foreign ultimately become one through the power of baptism.

Some General Conclusions about the Becket Legend

If the treatment of Gilbert Becket's bride shows significant variation across different versions, some important similarities and themes also emerge. The saint's future mother is not always a Saracen and, therefore, cannot be called a "Saracen princess." Nor does she always possess the same name; in fact, the kind of name she is given, Christian or non-Christian, changes with every new iteration of the legend. Even the level of importance granted the princess differs from one manifestation of the legend to the next: some versions place Thomas's mother on an equal footing with Gilbert Becket at the opening of the legend while others do not introduce her until Gilbert's capture, transforming her into a more romantic and less powerful figure in the process. What does not change in the portrayal of Thomas's mother is that she comes from the Middle East and that Gilbert Becket meets her as a result of his desire to go on pilgrimage. The account describing the encounter and union of Thomas Becket's parents in The *Later Quadrilogus*, *The South English Legendary*, the Middle English translation of the *Legenda Aurea*, and even the manuscript illuminations in the Queen Mary Psalter emphasizes the foreign identity of the princess at the same time that it highlights her essential role in the conception of England's "national" saint. In fact, it marks Thomas's mother as exceptional precisely because of her foreign nature. Having briefly discussed some of the most important medieval versions of Thomas Becket's origin legend, the time has now come to explore why this particular story gained so much popularity from the thirteenth century onwards and, indeed, why it was ever concocted at all.

To address this question, we must first consider the religious dimensions and implications of the narrative about Becket's non-Christian mother and why such a figure was deemed an improvement over Thomas's historical Anglo-Norman mother. This chapter began with an overview of historical accounts of Thomas's parentage, ones that emphasized that, far from issuing from illustrious stock, Thomas came from a rather ordinary Anglo-Norman family. However, this part of Thomas's narrative could have been revised and altered in a number of different ways. We must look, therefore, to what specific needs the legend responds in order the better to understand the use to which the foreign princess is put in this introduction to Thomas's life.

To begin, the narrative about a non-Christian woman converting to Christianity reflects Thomas's own journey from living in the world at the court of Henry II early in his career to dedicating his life to the church after his consecration as archbishop of Canterbury. Like the princess, Becket's journey began with materialistic concerns, and he only found his true vocation after satisfying his worldly ambitions. The parallels between Becket and his non-Christian mother of legend did not escape contemporary audiences and producers of the legend, as has been argued by Robert Mills. In discussing the Queen Mary Psalter images, for example, Mills notes the similarities in the illuminations depicting the princess's baptism and that of Thomas's consecration as archbishop of Canterbury:

> At folio 291r Thomas Becket himself is consecrated as archbishop...in a miniature clearly designed to echo the image showing his mother in the moment of her conversion: he assumes the same full-frontal pose and is again flanked by two bishops on either side. This serves to emphasize visually Becket's own status as a convert, from worldliness (as King Henry's chancellor) to his subsequent holiness (as prelate), a revolutionary turnaround that mirrors the transformation of his mother.[55]

The foreign princess of the Becket legend thus prefigures the saint's embodiment of both the worldly and the spiritual and his eventual conversion from a life lived in the world to the life of the spirit. At the same time, the princess also provides Thomas with a pedigree, both material and spiritual, missing from his rather pedestrian historical family background. For such a short narrative, the legend accomplishes much to bolster and heighten the saint's fame and promote his cult, and the figure of the foreign-born princess lies at the heart of this endeavor.

There exist other, larger issues to consider when attempting to explain the creation and dissemination of the legend about Thomas Becket's non-Christian mother in late medieval England. At the time of Thomas Becket's death, his ties to the Norman elite ruling England posed no obstacle to his identification as an English saint. By the time the first manifestations of the legend began to emerge about a century later, the socio-political climate of the island had changed considerably. While the Plantagenets still held sway over England, English men and women had begun to dissociate themselves from continental culture. Such a shift is visible in, for instance, the increased use of English—as opposed to French—as the medium for serious scholarly and literary works. Symptomatic of this important change, *The South English Legendary* reveals both a marked linguistic preference for English and definite "anti-Norman sentiments."[56] Such an observation leads Mills to conclude that "St. Thomas Becket's French-speaking heritage is subjected to a double erasure: not only is his father introduced as thoroughly rooted in England...but his mother is originally...the daughter of a powerful emir."[57] Mills's words suggest that the princess's identity is not as important as her non-identity: Thomas's mother can be pagan, Saracen, or Jewish, but she cannot be Norman.

---

55 Mills, "Invisible Translation," 141.
56 Mills, "The Early *South English Legendary* and Difference," 208.
57 Mills, "The Early *South English Legendary* and Difference," 209.

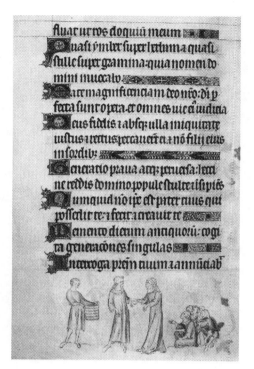

Figure 1: Bas-de-page scene of the mother of Thomas, the Saracen Emir's daughter, being recognized by Gilbert Becket's servant, London, British Library, Royal 2.B.VII, fol. 288v. Image courtesy of the British Library.

Figure 2: Detail of a bas-de-page of the mother of Thomas of Canterbury being baptized, immersed in a large font, by two bishops, London, British Library, Royal 2.B.VII, fol. 289r. Image courtesy of the British Library.

Figure 3: Bas-de-page scene of the mother of Thomas Becket, the Saracen Emir's daughter, being married to Gilbert Becket, London, British Library, Royal 2.B.VII, fol. 289v. Image courtesy of the British Library.

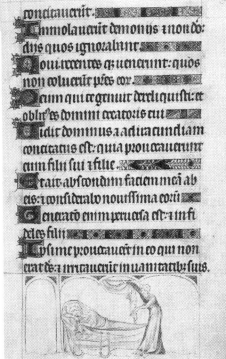

Figure 4: Bas-de-page scene of Thomas Becket's mother lying in bed with the infant Thomas beside her in a cradle and a woman holding back the curtain, London, British Library, Royal 2.B.VII, fol. 290r. Image courtesy of the British Library.

Yet, if we approach the Becket legend as a narrative influenced by the crusading movement—especially English participation in the Third Crusade—the princess's association with the Holy Land and her identity as an Eastern woman become critical. Katerina Hodges-Kluck describes one particular historical moment in crusading history that may have helped inspire the legend. In 1190, perhaps in the month of October, the archbishop of Canterbury, Baldwin, led English crusading troops brandishing an image of Thomas Becket into battle at Acre. After Baldwin's death, his successor in the office of archbishop of Canterbury, Hubert Walter, is believed to have founded a hospital in Acre dedicated to the English saint.[58] Soon thereafter, the Order of St. Thomas of Acre was founded, and, in 1227, the Knights of St. Thomas built the Hospital of St. Thomas of Acre in the parish of St. Mary Colechurch in London.[59] I would argue that Baldwin's decision to carry Thomas's banner into battle at Acre thus initiated a process that would eventually connect the Muslim world with Thomas Becket through his mother. The link made between Thomas and Acre may have led Englishmen and women, especially those confronted with the very real, very tangible presence of the Hospital of Thomas of Acre in the heart of London to inquire as to the root of this connection. The response that Thomas's mother came from the Holy Land may have seemed both simpler and more appealing than the truth. Thus, those individuals—for example, auditors of the Middle English translation of the *Legenda Aurea*—ignorant of the exact nature of the events of the Third Crusade may have satisfied their natural curiosity with a fictitious narrative about Thomas's mother.

We must also reflect on the trends regarding sainthood and hagiographical narratives from the thirteenth century onwards. In *Saints and Society: Christendom, 1000–1700*, Donald Weinstein and Rudolph M. Bell emphasize that saints' lives focusing on archbishops decreased in popularity at this time.[60] This shift in trend might have had an especially troublesome outcome on the legend and cult of Becket, whose quarrel with Henry II—and his consequent martyrdom at the hands of four of Henry's knights—derived directly from his position as archbishop of Canterbury, making Thomas the most powerful representative of the church in England from the time of his appointment to his death in 1170.

And what better way to inspire worshippers to believe in the cult of Becket than to assign to his life a literary motif associated with romances and *chansons de geste*? John Frankis has argued that *The South English Legendary* may have originally been composed by members of the secular clergy.[61] Were we to extend this hypothesis to the different versions of the legend and to speculate further that secular clergy were more likely to write for lay audiences than their non-secular counterparts, Thomas's mother may well have played an important role in the development of Thomas' cult.[62] That Thomas's mother

---

58 Kluck, "The Matter of Jerusalem," 66–67.

59 Warner, "Adventurous Custance," 44.

60 Donald Weinstein and Rudolph M. Bell, *Saints and Society: Christendom, 1000–1700* (Chicago: University of Chicago Press, 1982), 202–5.

61 Frankis, "The Social Context of Vernacular Writing," 78.

62 The inclusion of *King Horn* and *Havelok the Dane* in the Laud manuscript seems to reinforce the theory that *The South English Legendary* was intended at least in part for lay auditors.

leaves her father and community to follow Gilbert Becket to London renders Thomas's story more accessible to an audience accustomed to romance and marvel literature. By recalling other non-Christian princesses of romance and *chansons de geste*, Gilbert's bride might have functioned as a ploy to draw lay auditors into the story of Thomas's life.

As a whole, the legend is filled with paradoxes and contradictions. The conception of the saint results from both God's watchful guidance of the princess as she makes the arduous journey from her native land to London and her love for her father's English captive. Textually, the legend is also rife with contradictions, the spiritual preface to the life of England's greatest saint borrowing the literary motif of the Saracen princess of romance and *chanson de geste*. The legend even performs ambiguously as a politico-cultural tool: the tale of Gilbert and his lover distances Thomas from his historical Norman ancestry so as to reinforce his English identity, rewriting Thomas's Anglo-Norman mother as a non-Christian, Eastern woman. One might wonder why the tale of Becket's non-Christian mother endures beyond the fall of the last crusader state in 1291, lasting well into the modern period. In the end, the romantic tale of the foreign princess who journeys to England out of love for Gilbert Becket is simply a good story, a tale full of adventure, love, and suspense with the power to draw in audiences from a variety of cultural and social backgrounds.

The short account describing the encounter of Gilbert Becket with the non-Christian woman who will become Thomas's mother presents us with one last puzzle in its ambivalent approach to difference and conversion. At the beginning of the legend, the princess's difference, symbolized by her lack of knowledge of the English language, is given positive value, her inability to make her way to London of her own will proving the presence of God's guiding hand as she travels towards London and Gilbert Becket. Once the princess arrives in England, however, her lack of understanding of English becomes a problem, leading first to her humiliation by London mobs, then to Gilbert's perceived loss of freedom as a result of her dependence on him. It is to this narrative instability in the legend's portrayal of difference and the conversion of the non-Christian Other that I turn in the last pages of this chapter.

Becket's Mother, Conversion, and Racialization

The very same tale that presents Thomas as the divinely inspired product of a union between East and West, Christian and non-Christian, reveals anxiety about conversion by raising doubts about the assimilation of the Other, Thomas's non-Christian mother, into English, Christian society. In doing so, the text shows the same kind of hesitation about the integration of the baptized Other into Latin Christian society as *The King of Tars* and, especially, *Bevis of Hampton*. Once Thomas's future mother arrives in England, her difference—up to this point restricted to her faith as is the case with Bramimonde in the *Chanson de Roland*—becomes visible, her strangeness noted by the narrator and ridiculed by the citizens of London.[63] Even more poignantly, she continues to stand out

---

[63] Gilbert Becket is captured by a sultan rather than an Amiral in the fifteenth-century manuscript of *The South English Legendary* that presents the sultan and his daughter as Jewish.

after her conversion to Christianity and her marriage to Gilbert Becket, the unalienable truth of her alterity illustrated by her exchange with her husband when she finds out he wishes to return to the Holy Land to complete his pilgrimage. He cannot fulfill his desire, he explains, because he dares not leave her alone when she is so young and knows neither the customs nor the language of her new community. The two brief episodes describing the princess's arrival on English soil and her exchange with Gilbert after her baptism and marriage emphasize that the alterity of Thomas's mother is not limited purely to the religious and that her difference lingers after her baptism. Like another Josian, the princess does eventually become a good Christian—and English—lady, but her journey towards integration into English, Christian society persists beyond her arrival in London and her baptism.

The princess's transformation upon her arrival on English shores is both immediate and jarring. As Becket's mother is transported from a fantastical Eastern world to the familiar context of London, she metamorphoses from a figure of authority with tremendous power over Gilbert's life into a spectacle for jeering London crowds. In this moment, her difference, one that had not even been an object of note while she and Gilbert were in the Holy Land, displaces any and all other considerations the audience might have about her. Instead, the princess comes to embody alterity, her strength and determination forgotten or superimposed by her insurmountable, inexorable Otherness.

Only those, like the princess herself, who have crossed borders and inhabited both familiar and unfamiliar spaces, namely Gilbert Becket and the servant who accompanied him on his pilgrimage, still possess the ability to recognize her value. As was the case with Gilbert in the *Prise d'Orange*, Gilbert Becket and his man act as the intermediaries essential to bridging the two realms, familiar and Other. Where the men, women, and children of London, rooted in the local and the familiar, see the princess as a "best," Gilbert Becket and his servant can "read" the princess for what she truly is: a valuable commodity.

As such, the passage describing the princess's arrival in London could be understood as reinforcing the significance of Thomas's future mother, her difference only emphasized the further to highlight the miracle of her conversion and Thomas's conception. After all, not only do Gilbert and his man recognize and assist her, but she also receives the support of six bishops happening to meet at St. Paul's church, all this prior to being rewarded for her willingness to accept baptism with the hand of the man she loves. Her alterity, so powerful and all-consuming when she first lands in England, can now safely recede back into the shadows and vanish once again.

Except the difference that the non-Christian, foreign princess has come to represent does not disappear. Despite her recognition and approval by her lover, his companion, and the six bishops, despite her marriage to Gilbert, despite even her baptism, the princess remains decidedly Other, as is demonstrated in the exchange between Gilbert and his new bride that takes place after her conversion and marriage. Immediately after the wedding, Gilbert decides to return to the Holy Land to complete his pilgrimage, cut short earlier on in the narrative by his capture by the princess's father. However, Gilbert feels duty-bound to remain by his wife's side, in great part because he worries about her inability to speak English. When the princess finds out his secret wish to return to the Holy Land, she enjoins him to go on pilgrimage and not to worry about her as long as he leaves her with his servant, the man who accompanied him on his first pilgrimage and who, in several versions of the legend, first recognizes the princess upon her arrival in England. This man knows her language and can serve as her interpreter and translator, the princess reminds her husband. Here, I would like to stress that this episode is not, strictly speaking, required to conclude the narrative. Not only has the princess already converted to Christianity, but she and Gilbert have also married and conceived Thomas. At first glance, the passage thus takes the guise of an unnecessary quota to an otherwise complete legend.

If the princess has already received baptism and conceived her saintly son, why include this passage at all? I would argue that the brief exchange between Gilbert and his wife in fact achieves three important goals. First, it further establishes and reinforces Gilbert as a deeply religious man. In the process of re-affirming this aspect of Gilbert's character, the episode gives the legend narrative symmetry by mirroring Gilbert's first expedition to the Holy Land at the opening of the account. As Shokoofeh Rajabzadeh has shown, this mirroring occurs on several levels with Gilbert returning to the Holy Land at the same time that he and the princess trade places.

Second, the end of the narrative parallels its beginnings. This time, instead of Gilbert, Alisaundre Becket is isolated in a space. And instead of Alisaundre, Gilbert travels in and out of the space freely. However, unlike the beginning of the narrative, where Alisaundre was unburdened by language, language poses the primary obstacle to Gilbert's movement.[64]

While the narrative concludes with the repetition and completion of Gilbert Becket's eastern voyage, the nature of the obstacles confronting Gilbert and the princess have changed considerably. Superficially, Gilbert seems to have gained in freedom and in his ability to penetrate foreign lands; in reality, the princess, though hindered by a persistent lack of cultural and linguistic understanding of English society, manages her new environment competently and successfully while the anxiety of her conversion and assimilation rests on Gilbert's shoulders and hampers his freedom of movement.

Third and more importantly, the exchange between Thomas Becket's newlywed parents highlights the princess's private transformation into a Christian burgher's wife. Although I would not go so far as Rajabzadeh in arguing that the princess's foreign tongue "racializes" her, the author(s) of the legend seems at pains to show both that "conversion to Christianity does not automatically erase, change, or reorient all of one's identity markers" and that—since most versions of the legend end when Gilbert returns from his second pilgrimage to find his wife fully integrated into English society—assimilation does eventually follow upon conversion.[65] As Robert Mills puts it:

> These references to acts of interlingual transfer articulate a layer of language activity that is more commonly occluded in medieval literature…What at the outset is effaced—the experience of cultural exchange across linguistic borders—becomes, in conclusion, a discernible presence: the translator enters the scene.[66]

---

64 Rajabzadeh, "Alisaundre Becket," 299.
65 Rajabzadeh, "Alisaundre Becket," 299.
66 Mills, "Invisible Translation," 133.

Why render "discernible" "what at the outset is effaced"?[67] Why call attention to the fact that the princess's "conversion to Christianity does not automatically erase, change, or reorient" her difference, only to show her to have successfully assimilated into English society by the end of the account?[68] Where the *Chanson de Roland* and the *Prise d'Orange* conclude with the climactic baptism of a Saracen woman to Christianity, the Becket legend does not—perhaps cannot—end with the princess's baptism, her marriage, or even the conception of the saintly Thomas. Instead, the legend shows the need to note both that the princess remains different after her conversion and that she does eventually succeed in adapting to English society, this by the time Gilbert returns home from his pilgrimage three and a half years later.

In its dual celebration and fear of alterity as well as in its emphatic assertion that baptism does not erase difference completely—in fact, to any significant degree—the Becket legend approaches conversion in much the same way as *Bevis of Hampton*. Like Josian, Gilbert's bride turns to a liminal figure, Gilbert's servant and erstwhile Eastern companion, to navigate her new Christian world in her lover's absence. Like Josian also, Becket's mother needs time to complete her transformation from a heathen princess into a virtuous Christian lady. Although we are not told the exact duration of this process, the fact that three and a half years pass before Thomas's mother becomes indistinguishable from other Christian noblewomen indicates that time is required before one can truly integrate the Christian community. In both *Bevis of Hampton* and the Becket legend, baptism is only the beginning.

Despite the need for Thomas Becket's mother to hail from without the Christian world, the Becket legend ultimately aligns itself with the fourteenth-century *King of Tars* and *Bevis of Hampton* in its concern with both religious and socio-cultural characteristics in identifying and distinguishing the Other. Moreover, one might argue the legend privileges the socio-cultural over the purely religious. Although *The King of Tars* initially points to socio-cultural customs and habits in its treatment of the false conversion of the princess of Tars, the poem eventually re-asserts the climactic and all-consuming power of baptism when the princess's husband, the Sultan of Damascus, converts to Christianity. By contrast, the Becket legend provides Thomas Becket with a fictitious non-Christian mother only to problematize her alterity in the second half of the narrative. As with *Bevis of Hampton*, the Becket legend complicates the interaction between Christian and non-Christian, both celebrating and alienating those without the Christian *communitas*. These two texts stress that baptism is neither the sole nor the more powerful factor in determining difference and that alterity remains deeply rooted in the Other beyond conversion to Christianity. Are the Becket legend and *Bevis of Hampton* alone in their approach to conversion or does the power of baptism likewise diminish in other late medieval English works? This is the next question we must address, one that leads us directly to Chaucer's *Man of Law's Tale*.

---

67 Mills, "Invisible Translation," 133.
68 Rajabzadeh, "Alisaundre Becket," 299.

Chapter 3

THE BECKET LEGEND, *THE MAN OF LAW'S TALE*, AND CONVERSION

The suspicion of non-Christians seeking baptism that begins to emerge in the Becket legend and *Bevis of Hampton*, among other late medieval English works, is accentuated in Geoffrey Chaucer's *Man of Law's Tale*. In Chaucer's retelling of the story of the pure, exiled Christian princess Constance, non-Christians such as the Sultaness, the Sultan of Syria's mother, feign the desire to convert the better to entrap their Christian victims.

The stark treatment of non-Christians in *The Man of Law's Tale* and the narrative's dismissal of baptism as a life-altering ritual are rendered even more meaningful by the knowledge that Chaucer knew the Becket legend. To emphasize the connection between the two texts, the first section of this chapter stresses the varied ways in which *The Man of Law's Tale* both echoes and responds to the legend about Becket's non-Christian mother. Having made this argument, I examine the portrayal and function of conversion in *The Man of Law's Tale*, highlighting the similarities in the two narratives. In this second part of the chapter, I look particularly at how the two tales differentiate between the Other and the familiar while also signaling an important shift in the thematic treatment of conversion in Chaucer's tale.

The Becket Legend and *The Man of Law's Tale*

The connection between the Becket legend and Geoffrey Chaucer's *The Man of Law's Tale* was first established over eighty years ago by Paul Alonzo Brown. In his 1930 study, *The Development of the Legend of Thomas Becket*, Brown emphasized the influence of the Saracen princess motif on the legend.[1] More recently, Lawrence Warner has convincingly argued that the legend provides both an etiological origin for the Order of St. Thomas of Acre—giving Becket a non-Christian mother so as to explain his association with Acre—and a secondary source for Chaucer's retelling of the Constance narrative.[2] However, neither Brown nor Warner have analyzed the extent to which Chaucer is responding to and retelling the story of Thomas Becket's mother. Nor does either author consider what a juxtaposition of the legend with *The Man of Law's Tale* might reveal about the latter, particularly when considering the place of conversion in these and other fourteenth-century English narratives.

At first, Chaucer's *Man of Law's Tale* seems to possess very little in common with the Becket legend. A rewriting of Nicholas Trivet's story of Constance in *The Anglo-Norman Chronicles* that probably also bears the influence of Chaucer's contemporary, John Gower, and his own version of the Constance narrative, *The Man of Law's Tale* tells the story of a virtuous Roman princess buffeted by God from one foreign shore to another on a rudderless boat. Where the Saracen princess motif does not appear in the tales of

---

1 Brown, *The Development of the Legend of Thomas Becket*, 51–65.
2 Warner, "Adventurous Custance," 51.

Chaucer, Gower, and Trivet, this trope plays a crucial role in the Becket legend, as noted in the previous chapter.[3] The heroine of Chaucer's tale, like those of Trivet and Gower, is very much a Christian princess meant to spread the message of Christ to the men she marries and their subjects.

Yet, if we look a little deeper, there exist undeniable similarities between the two tales. In "Adventurous Custance: St. Thomas of Acre and Chaucer's *Man of Law's Tale*," Lawrence Warner identifies three primary elements shared by both narratives: 1) both Gilbert Becket and King Alla of Northumbria, Custance's second husband, leave their wives almost immediately after conceiving a son; 2) both Becket's Saracen mother and Custance travel by ship to England; and 3) the narrative includes a crucial meeting with several bishops.[4] Of these three shared components, the most significant is undoubtedly the second one: travel by ship. In *The Man of Law's Tale*, Custance's lengthy voyage highlights her suffering and faith while also serving as a metaphor for the soul's turbulent journey through life.[5] As for the Thomas legend, it presents the Saracen princess's arduous journey as the essential step that will transform her from a heroine of romance into the virtuous mother of England's greatest saint. In both narratives, the heroine's suffering at sea is paired with faith in God, whose guidance allows for the character to survive and ultimately overcome all obstacles.

In addition to the three commonalities between *The Man of Law's Tale* and the Becket legend identified by Lawrence Warner, the legend and *The Man of Law's Tale* are further linked by the emphasis on marriage as a step necessary to the conversion of heathens and by the significance placed on women as the producers of famous sons. In its use of marriage and love as a tool for the conversion of heathens, both texts utilize elements found in *chansons de geste* and romances from the twelfth century onwards. According to Jennifer Goodman, such interest in interreligious marriages also points to the significance of women in converting the Other to Christianity.[6] That marriage between Christians and heathens is portrayed as climactic in both tales thus aligns itself with various medieval approaches to the Muslim world and the question of conversion.

In the primary role assigned to Custance and Thomas's mother, the two narratives diverge more clearly from most medieval works concerned with the founding of a famous lineage. Where most such accounts focus on the male founders of a famous line, both *The Man of Law's Tale* and the Becket legend privilege matrilineal heritage. In the case of Thomas's mother, the princess's arrival in London and her marriage to Gilbert Becket herald the conception of the future saint, and Thomas's birth hinges on the successful completion of his mother's journey. The significance of Custance to the founding of a new

---

3 Brown, *The Development of the Legend of Thomas Becket*, 51–65.

4 Warner, "Adventurous Custance," 52–53.

5 In "The Tale and Its Teller: The Case of Chaucer's Man of Law," Kevin J. Harty states that "she spends upwards of eight years in the tale adrift at sea, a common enough metaphor for life's uncertainties." Kevin J. Harty, "The Tale and Its Teller: The Case of Chaucer's Man of Law," *The American Benedictine Review*, 34, no. 4 (1983): 365.

6 Jennifer R. Goodman, "Marriage and Conversion in Late Medieval Romance," in *Varieties of Religious Conversion*, ed. James Muldoon (Gainesville: University of Florida Press, 1997), 115–28.

line of Christian leaders is perhaps less heavily highlighted in *The Man of Law's Tale*. Yet, here also, Custance serves as the crucial link between her father, the Roman emperor, Alla, her second, Northumbrian husband, and the next generation of Christian princes uniting the Saxon tribes and the Roman Empire in the person of Maurice, her son.[7] Both the legend about Becket's mother and *The Man of Law's Tale* thus underscore the significance of marriage in bringing about heathen conversion to Christianity and the function of women in effecting such conversions and in creating powerful new lineages.

One last commonality linking the Becket legend to Chaucer's *Man of Law's Tale* lies in the heroines' inability to communicate effectively upon arrival in England, a point debated by scholars in the case of Chaucer's piece because it marks a departure from his immediate source, Trivet's tale of Constance. In "'But algates therby was she understonde': Translating Custance in Chaucer's *Man of Law's Tale*," Christine F. Cooper summarizes the problem:

> As a number of scholars have noted, in having Custance speak Latin Chaucer has made an important change from his source, the fourteenth-century Anglo-Norman *Les Cronicles* of Nicholas Trevet: rather than being learned in many languages and able to speak Saxon to the constable, Custance speaks only her own language, which is nevertheless understood by the Northumbrians…In contrast to Trevet's educated woman who can speak Saxon, Chaucer's Custance is a monolingual Latin speaker who can communicate only by having her language understood by the Saxon Northumbrians.

> Many critics have attempted to explain why Chaucer alters Custance's language abilities. Some, including J. A. Burrow and A. C. Spearing, argue that Chaucer was trying for "historical verisimilitude" by reflecting what he understood to be the early medieval linguistic situation as Latin evolved from classical to "corrupt" Latin or Italian, as spoken in Italy or possibly throughout Europe as the "lingua franca" of merchants. Others assert that Chaucer intended the mention of "corrupt Latin" to signal a significant language barrier between Custance and the early British, and that it therefore serves a thematic purpose by reflecting on Custance's character and/or heightening her experience of vulnerability and outsidedness.[8]

Likewise puzzled by Chaucer's divergence from his primary source, Shayne Aaron Legassie claims that:

> To understand Custance's Italian dialect, Olda makes do with the available scraps, the scattered, vestigial ligaments that link England-weakly and unsystematically-to Latinate culture. Admittedly, the "Man of Law's Tale" does not explicitly account for how this linguistic gap is bridged, but the very notion of Custance's vernacular as a "maner of Latyn corrupt" recalls the medieval tendency to explain linguistic kinship and difference in terms of the rise and fall of empires and the schema of salvation history.[9]

---

7 Nicholas Birns, "'To Aleppo Gone': From the North Sea to Syria in Chaucer's *Man of Law's Tale* and Shakespeare's *Macbeth*," *Exemplaria*, 24, no. 4 (Winter 2012): 378 and Heng, *Empire of Magic*, 182, 209, as cited in Kathy Cawsey, "Disorienting Orientalism: Finding Saracens in Strange Places in Late Medieval English Manuscripts," *Exemplaria*, 21, no. 4 (Winter 2009): 390.

8 Cooper, "'But algates therby was she understonde': Translating Custance in Chaucer's *Man of Law's Tale*," *The Yearbook of English Studies*, 36, no. 1 (2006): 29–30.

9 Shayne Aaron Legassie, "Among Other Possible Things: The Cosmopolitanisms of Chaucer's *Man of Law's Tale*," in *Cosmopolitanism and the Middle Ages*, ed. John M. Ganim (New York: Palgrave,

This aspect of Chaucer's tale, however, can be elucidated through a juxtaposition with the Becket legend. Chaucer diverges from his immediate sources, particularly Nicholas Trivet and John Gower, because of his reliance on the legend at this juncture. In doing so, I would argue that Chaucer has two ends in mind. First, he emphasizes Custance's linguistic vulnerability so as to highlight her lack of control and her complete dependence on God—just as the legend depicts Thomas's mother as unable to communicate on her own to stress the role of God in the conception of Thomas. Like Thomas's birth, Custance's conversion of the heathen Alla is wholly contingent on God's will and guidance. Second, Chaucer chooses to underline Custance's inability to speak other languages precisely to remind his contemporary audience of the legend about Thomas Becket's mother.

That Chaucer seeks to make his heroine more vulnerable to prove the power of God aligns itself well with conventional interpretations of the tale according to which the Man of Law attempts to contribute a Christian perspective on the debate about Fate and Free Will developed in the First Fragment. As V. A. Kolve has argued, Custance is here presented as the "Ship of the Church Militant" and her surrender of her life and fate to God exemplifies ideal Christian behaviour.[10] To provide Custance with a knowledge of languages would equate to giving her at least partial control over her destiny and would, thereby, diminish the tale's message about God's supreme power. At the same time, however, Custance's complete dependence on God does present a significant divergence from Nicholas Trivet's and John Gower's versions of the Constance narrative. Chaucer here seems to direct his audience's attention away from his primary sources, texts he otherwise follows fairly closely. By using a motif that serves an essential function in the Becket legend, Chaucer links his tale with the earlier narrative.[11]

Linguistically, the connection between Custance and Thomas's mother—particularly the manner in which their lack of speech is described—is less than obvious. The only words to be used both by Chaucer and the anonymous author(s) of the Becket legend—at least in most of the manuscripts preserved—is the phrase "in hir langage."[12] Both heroines are shown to speak and understand a language different and distinct from English. However, the Becket legend stresses the Otherness of the foreign princess seeking Gilbert Becket. The focus is not on the foreign language she speaks, but, rather, on her inability to communicate in English. The narrative goes on to describe the reactions of London burghers, including children, to the linguistically Othered princess. Because she

---

2013), 191.

10 V. A. Kolve, as cited in Warner, "Adventurous Custance," 50.

11 That Chaucer and his audience knew the legend is clear. According to Lawrence Warner, Chaucer would have had several opportunities to be exposed to the legend. Nor did one have to be educated or even literate to know of this story, one circulated particularly amongst the merchants—especially mercers—who claimed St. Thomas of Acre as their patron saint. One can infer both that Chaucer knew the legend and that he likewise expected his contemporary audience to have some familiarity with it. Warner, "Adventurous Custance," 51.

12 *The Early South-English Legendary*, lines 62 and 131. This particular phrase is not found in the version of the legend in *The South English Legendary*. However, both editions—and the different manuscripts on which they are based—emphasize the princess's inability to speak English from the moment she decides to leave her native land to follow Gilbert Becket.

cannot speak English, she appears to them as a dehumanized, if entertaining, creature and a marvel to laugh at.[13]

On the contrary, Chaucer highlights a different aspect of Custance's linguistic difference. Unlike the anonymous creator(s) of the Becket legend, Chaucer spends little time describing the Northumbrian constable's reaction to the effectively speechless Custance. In fact, the only person to find Custance "strange" (foreign) in Northumbria is Donegild, Alla's mother.[14] Rather, Chaucer focuses on labeling Custance's language, identifying it as "a maner Latyn corrupt" (Latin...of a degenerate kind).[15]

Where the two narratives do converge is in their approach to their heroine, presented as powerless in both the Becket legend and *The Man of Law's Tale*. In the legend, the princess's vulnerability is conveyed externally when the reader is provided brief insight into the minds of the gaping London crowd who equate her lack of English with beastliness. As Robert Mills suggests, she is dehumanized in the process, transformed into an abject victim until Gilbert Becket finds her.[16] Although Chaucer's focus remains on Custance while describing her monolingualism, he also vividly conveys his heroine's complete victimization: what she requests "in hir langage" (in her foreign language) is for the constable to kill her so as to end her suffering.[17] Custance and Becket's mother are thus portrayed as hapless victims of Fate lacking any control over their lives, a point emphasized in both narratives by the women's inability to speak English or, in fact, anything aside from "hir langage."[18] It is worth noting that this linguistic helplessness does not manifest itself until the narratives' respective heroines, Becket's non-Christian mother and Custance, have reached England, as if the confrontation of the fantasy, imaginary Eastern world they represent with the real and the familiar forces the realization of their difference, their unmitigated Otherness.

So far, I have discussed commonalities that link the Becket legend with Chaucer's *Man of Law's Tale*, but there exist important differences between the two narratives that, paradoxically, further reinforce the connections between the two works. One significant difference distinguishing the Becket legend from *The Man of Law's Tale* lies in the will of the heroine. In both narratives, God arranges for a heathen to marry a Christian, a union that will result in the conversion of the heathen partner and the birth of an exceptional child. However, whereas Thomas Becket's mother hopes and labours for such a union, Custance merely gives herself up to the will of God, and her lack of will manifests itself on several occasions in *The Man of Law's Tale*. Unlike Becket's mother in the thirteenth-

---

[13] Mills, "Conversion, Translation and Becket's 'heathen' Mother," 389.

[14] *The Man of Law's Tale*, line 700. Throughout the rest of this study, I will be using Larry D. Benson's edition of *The Canterbury Tales* and Nevill Goghill's translation. Geoffrey Chaucer, *The Riverside Chaucer*, ed. Larry D. Benson, 3rd ed. (Boston: Houghton, 1987); Geoffrey Chaucer, *The Canterbury Tales*, trans. Nevill Coghill (1971; repr., London: Penguin, 2003), 159.

[15] *The Man of Law's Tale*, line 519; Chaucer, *The Canterbury Tales*, 154.

[16] Mills, "Conversion, Translation and Becket's 'heathen' Mother," 387–88.

[17] *The Man of Law's Tale*, line 516; Chaucer, *The Canterbury Tales*, 154.

[18] *The Man of Law's Tale*, line 516; Chaucer, *The Canterbury Tales*, 154.

century legend, Custance takes no action to seek England out; in fact, she wishes only to stay in Rome.

When Custance finally does arrive in England, it is because she has been led to meet Alla and convert him and his subjects. Their marriage is arranged by God, and it is unclear whether either Alla or Custance even want to enter into this union. The lack of romance and feeling between the two partners is conveyed in the brief lines that describe Alla's marriage to Custance:

> And after this Jhesus, of his mercy,
> Made Alla wedden ful solempnely
> This hooly mayden, that is so bright and sheene
> And thus hath Crist ymaad Custance a queene.[19]

> Then Jesus in his mercy caused the King
> To wed this holy maiden. Belfries ring
> In solemn joy, and Constance the serene
> By ordinance of Christ is made a queen.[20]

It is not just Custance that is forced to enter this union, but also Alla, who is "made" to "wedden" Custance by Jesus. That Custance returns home to Rome at the conclusion of the tale also highlights her lack of personal commitment to her union with Alla. Unlike other medieval characters, Christian and non-Christian alike, that marry pagans, Custance's relationship with Alla does not override her other longings and needs: she remains with Alla while he is alive but only achieves full happiness when he dies and she is allowed to return to Rome. Where the Becket legend adopts the motif of the Saracen princess, Chaucer's Man of Law rejects the need for romantic love as a step towards turning to the divine.[21]

Moreover, unlike in the Becket legend, *The Man of Law's Tale* converges entirely and completely on Custance. Whereas the legend about Becket's parents serves as a precursor to the life of Thomas, the Man of Law presents Custance as his one and only hero. This claim is reinforced at the end of the tale when the Man of Law alludes to the important role to be played by Maurice, the son of Custance and Alla, only to dismiss him with the line "But I lete al his storie passen by" (My memories are dim).[22] Maurice never becomes the focal point of the narrative, and his mother's story matters not because it leads to his conception and birth but because of her own significance. Once again, *The Man of Law's Tale* diverges from the Becket legend in its emphatic focus on the mother rather than her illustrious offspring.

These points of distinction are significant because they suggest that Chaucer consciously engages with the Becket legend in *The Man of Law's Tale*. In renouncing the

---

[19] *The Man of Law's Tale*, lines 690–93.

[20] Chaucer, *The Canterbury Tales*, 159.

[21] Kathy Cawsey has argued that the failed conversion of Syria in *The Man of Law's Tale* "suggest[s] that the Syrians or men of Barbary converted for the wrong reasons, and that is why their conversion was unsuccessful; the Northumbrians, by contrast, converted for the 'right' reasons." Cawsey, "Disorienting Orientalism," 390.

[22] *The Man of Law's Tale*, line 1124; Chaucer, *The Canterbury Tales*, 171.

motif of the Saracen princess and the concept that romantic love can bring a heathen closer to God, *The Man of Law's Tale* presents its readers with different ways of imagining "the conflict of opposing religious 'laws'" while also returning to a more pious, less secular approach to the genre of the saint's life.[23] As prominent Chaucerians such as A. C. Spearing have argued, here Chaucer privileges the genre of the saint's life over the romance. In doing so, however, Chaucer once again both aligns himself with and diverges from the popular legend about Becket. Both narratives use romance elements as a ploy to lure their audiences into stories about the exemplary lives of saintly figures: The legend utilizes romance elements to introduce Becket's life, and *The Man of Law's Tale* initially assumes the guise of a romance the better to focus on the saintly life of its heroine. It is important to note, however, that the Becket legend is presumed to function as a saint's life while *The Man of Law's Tale* is not. Expected to perform as a saint's life, the Becket legend instead draws on romance conventions; Chaucer, by contrast, infuses a hagiographic narrative into a tale believed to be and presented as romance. Chaucer is thus combining romance and hagiography in a similar fashion to the anonymous composer(s) of the Becket legend while also drawing in listeners with the use of the genre of the saint's life rather than away from it. While the Becket legend can be described as a saint's life diluted with romance elements, *The Man of Law's Tale* is disguised as a romance to underscore the importance of hagiographic narratives. Chaucer, it seems, is closing the loop opened by the Becket legend: where the anonymous creators of the legend took the story of Thomas—at least in its prologue—out of the genre to which it naturally belonged, Chaucer brings the saint's life back to the fore in *The Man of Law's Tale*.

The movement of the characters—particularly Custance—in *The Man of Law's Tale* further indicates that Chaucer engages with the Becket legend throughout his own narrative. In the legend, Gilbert Becket is brought to the princess who then follows him to England to marry him and conceive the saintly Thomas. In contrast, Custance is brought to England to marry Alla and conceive Maurice with him. After her departure from England, Alla follows her to Rome. *The Man of Law's Tale* tells the same basic story as the Becket legend, but with the main roles ascribed to different genders: the saintly, if rather passive, Christian male hero of the legend is replaced by a saintly, passive Christian female heroine in *The Man of Law's Tale*. From this perspective, Custance seems to initiate a saintly journey that will be mirrored and concluded by Thomas's mother in the Becket legend.

Despite several important differences between *The Man of Law's Tale* and the Becket legend, Chaucer's narrative in fact echoes, complements, and responds to the legend in a number of interesting ways. But what does this say about conversion in the tale? It is this question that we must now address.

---

23 Kathryn L. Lynch, "Storytelling, Exchange, and Constancy: East and West in Chaucer's *Man of Law's Tale*," The Chaucer Review, 33, no. 4 (1999): 409–10 and A. C. Spearing, "Narrative Voice: The Case of Chaucer's *Man of Law's Tale*," New Literary History, 32, no. 3 (Summer 2001): 739.

Conversion in *The Man of Law's Tale*

The Man of Law's Tale is rife with anxiety about conversion. Just as in the *Chanson de Roland*, Christian belief in the good faith of the Other in accepting baptism leads the Christian hero—in this case, heroine—to harm. The similarities between the *Chanson de Roland* and *The Man of Law's Tale* end there, however, and the message conveyed about conversion in Chaucer's tale differs significantly from that with which the famous twelfth-century *chanson de geste* concludes. Where the *Chanson de Roland* privileges faithful conversion through the climactic baptism of Queen Bramimonde, *The Man of Law's Tale* concludes with Custance's safe return home, an ending that raises intriguing questions about the value ascribed to conversion and missionary activity in the tale. At the same time—and despite agreeing with his central argument linking the Becket legend with *The Man of Law's Tale*—I question Lawrence Warner's claim that Chaucer "aligns his tale with crusading and mercantile energies."[24] Rather than providing a clear distinction between Christian and Muslim, friend and foe, I will argue over the next few pages that Chaucer's tale in fact highlights the disturbing *likeness* between Syrians and Northumbrians in his tale, one that renders both crusading and missionizing problematic.

Custance's initial adventures in Syria offer a nightmarish vision of conversion, one that relishes the threat posed to Latin Christendom by the missionary ideal. In this first episode, Chaucer seems to portray any union between Latin Christendom and Islam as hopeless. Even after the Sultan of Syria has decided to accept baptism and to convert his subjects to Christianity, Fate ordains otherwise, and the country reverts to its Islamic faith through the treachery of the Sultaness's mother, who kills her son and sends Custance adrift on her ship. Despite his genuine readiness to embrace Christianity, the Sultan of Syria is incapable of spreading the Christian faith, and his baptism only leads to his death. At this point in the tale, baptism is presented as completely ineffective, the non-Christian status of the Syrians re-established almost immediately after the supposedly momentous event of the sultan's baptism.

One of the most important scholars to have written on *The Man of Law's Tale* in the past twenty-five years, Susan Schibanoff, embraces the view that conversion is impotent and that the Syrians cannot be made into Christians. In "Worlds Apart: Orientalism, Antifeminism, and Heresy in Chaucer's *Man of Law's Tale*," Schibanoff argues that the Man of Law uses his tale to mediate amongst his fellow male pilgrims.[25] For Schibanoff,

---

[24] Lawrence, "Adventurous Custance," 49.

[25] Susan Schibanoff, "Worlds Apart: Orientalism, Antifeminism, and Heresy in Chaucer's *Man of Law's Tale*," *Exemplaria*, 8, no.1 (1996): 59–96. Since the publication of Schibanoff's piece, several scholars have felt the need to address her work. Kathryn L. Lynch, for example, challenges Schibanoff's primary thesis about the Orientalism inherent to *The Man of Law's Tale* and the Othering project undertaken by the Man of Law. Others seek to refine Schibanoff's thesis. For example, Kathleen Davis claims that *The Man of Law's Tale*'s "Orientalist discourse works *through*, rather than in addition to, its discourse on women." Yet others have been inspired by Susan Schibanoff's work to approach *The Man of Law's Tale* from analogous perspectives. Lawrence Warner and Siobhain Bly Calkin, for example, tackle the issue of crusading in Chaucer's tale, arguing that Chaucer's Man of Law explores crusading ideals in his tale. Another school of thought emphasizes the cosmopolitanism of *The Man of Law's Tale*. Shayne Aaron Legassie and Nicholas Birns read *The Man of Law's Tale*

the Man of Law seeks to attenuate the tension introduced by the Knight and "reorients the direction of *The Canterbury Tales*, heading it for the first time towards its pilgrimage goal."[26] The Man of Law wishes to unite the men on the pilgrimage by evoking a cause behind which they can all rally. To this end, the Man of Law tells a story in which English men such as Alla are depicted as strong and righteous while Saracen men, the Sultan and his followers, and women, the Sultaness and Custance's second, Northumbrian mother-in-law Donegild, are set up as negative foils. By the end of the tale, Schibanoff concludes, the Man of Law has succeeded in uniting the male pilgrims against all Others, particularly Saracens and women.[27]

The Sultaness, the Syrian woman Othered by gender and religion both in Schibanoff's reading of *The Man of Law's Tale*, is frightening not only because of her treachery and her ruthlessness but also on account of her approach to baptism. After concocting and explaining her evil plan to her followers, she urges them to accept baptism the better to deceive the Sultan:

> "We shul first feyne us cristendom to take—
> Coold water shal nat greve us but a lite!
> And I shal swich a feeste and revel make
> That, as I trowe, I shal the Sowdan quite.
> For, thogh his wyf be cristned never so white,
> She shal have nede to wasshe awey the rede,
> Thogh she a font-ful water with hire lede."[28]

> "We first must make pretence to be baptized
> —Cold water cannot hurt us very much—
> Thereafter let a feast be organized
> To pay the Sultan out, if he should touch.
> Though christened white, his wife and many such
> Shall find there's blood to wash away! She'll want
> More water than it takes to fill a font."[29]

as an attempt to associate England with the cosmopolitan courts of the Mediterranean. Along with Kathy Lavezzo, Legassie notes that Chaucer tries to provide as detailed an account of Custance's sea journey as possible, specifying that her boat goes from the Mediterranean Sea to England via the strait of Gibraltar. Lavezzo and Legassie both note that this attempt to make Custance's journey slightly more realistic diverges from Chaucer's immediate sources. Such arguments suggest that *The Man of Law's Tale* can be read, at least in part, as a declaration of the strength and power of England, a country presented as intimately connected to the courts of Rome and Syria despite its geographical distance from such medieval centres of culture and civilization. Lynch, "Storytelling, Exchange, and Constancy"; Kathleen Davis, "Time Behind the Veil: The Media, the Middle Ages, and Orientalism Now," in *The Postcolonial Middle Ages*, ed. Jeffrey Jerome Cohen (New York: St. Martin's, 2000), 116; Warner, "Adventurous Custance," 49; Siobhain Bly Calkin, "*The Man of Law's Tale* and Crusade," in *Medieval Latin and Middle English Literature: Essays in Honour of Jill Mann*, ed. Christopher Cannon and Maura Nolan (Woodbridge: Brewer, 2011), 2–3; Birns, "'To Aleppo Gone'"; Kathy Lavezzo, "Beyond Rome: Mapping Gender and Justice in *The Man of Law's Tale*," *Studies in the Age of Chaucer* 24 (2002): 149–80 at 152; and Legassie, "Among Other Possible Things," 197.

26 Schibanoff, "Worlds Apart," 60.
27 Schibanoff, "Worlds Apart," 95.
28 *The Man of Law's Tale*, lines 351–57.
29 Chaucer, *The Canterbury Tales*, 149.

In describing baptism as merely "coold water," the Sultaness diminishes the power of conversion and one of the holiest of Christian sacraments, reducing this rich ritual, one that plays a climactic role in so many earlier romances and *chansons de geste* to its most basic, elemental component.

This impression is reinforced at the end of the Sultaness's speech when she implicitly compares the thickness of the murdered converts' blood to baptismal water. The image conjured, that of a bloody Custance unable to wash away the blood of the Sultan and his followers, leaves no doubt as to the relative potency of the two liquids. Custance will be stained red, her baptism unable to wash away the horror that is to come. In this address to her followers, the Sultaness conveys a potent and chilling message about conversion to Christianity: baptism is only significant if those who convert will it to possess greater meaning. Otherwise, baptism and conversion to Christianity are no more than a harmless sprinkling of water.

Despite this bleak attitude to baptism and conversion, the Syrian episode reveals itself to possess far more ambiguity. To begin with, the Syrian Other supplies the narrative with both Christian martyrs and their heathen tormentors in *The Man of Law's Tale*: if the Sultaness reverts to the Muslim faith, her son dies a Christian. One cannot read the sultaness as a cruel, treacherous pagan executioner without also reading the Sultan as her victim and a martyr to his new faith.

Moreover, as has been pointed out by numerous scholars, Custance's adventures in Northumbria bear a striking resemblance to those she encountered in Syria. In fact, the correlations between the Syrian and Northumbrian episodes are abundant. Alla's name, for example, is reminiscent of the Muslim name for God.[30] The similitude existing between the Sultan's mother and Donegild, Alla's mother, both of whom reject and attempt to destroy Custance because of her difference, has also been noted.[31] Such details suggest that conversion is not merely problematic in Syria and that the distinction between Syrians and Northumbrians is not as clear as Schibanoff implies.

Geraldine Heng has argued in *Empire of Magic* that the Northumbrian episode diverges from its Syrian predecessor in one essential way: Custance's union to the Sultan is never consummated but that between Custance and Alla immediately produces a child, Maurice. According to Heng, it is no accident that Custance bears a perfect male child to Alla and not the Sultan, and Heng looks to *The King of Tars* to suggest that any child resulting from Custance's union to her first husband would have, like the offspring of the Sultan of Damascus and the princess of Tars, been born insensate and lifeless.[32]

---

[30] As noted by Anthony Bale, Kathy Cawsey, Kathryn L. Lynch, and Nicholas Birns, amongst others. Anthony Bale, "'A maner Latyn corrupt': Chaucer and the Absent Religions," in *Chaucer and Religion*, ed. Helen Phillips (Woodbridge: Brewer, 2010), 63; Cawsey, "Disorienting Orientalism," 388; Lynch, "Storytelling, Exchange, and Constancy," 417; and Birns, "'To Aleppo Gone,'" 366–67.

[31] See especially Elizabeth Robertson, "The 'Elvyssh' Power of Constance: Christian Feminism in Geoffrey Chaucer's *The Man of Law's Tale*," *Studies in the Age of Chaucer* 23 (2001): 143–80 at 155; Cawsey, "Disorienting Orientalism," 388; and Marjorie Elizabeth Wood, "The Sultaness, Donegild, and Fourteenth-Century Female Merchants," *Comitatus: A Journal of Medieval and Renaissance Studies* 37 (2006): 65–85 at 84.

[32] Heng, *Empire of Magic*, 227–28. Heng notes that Donegild invents a monstrous child, but

Yet, despite the fact that the union of Custance and the Sultan remains unconsummated, the monstrous child does appear in *The Man of Law's Tale*, manifesting itself in the child fabricated by Donegild in her counterfeit message to her son:

> The lettre spak the queene delivered was
> Of so horrible a feendly creature
> That in the castel noon so hardy was
> That any while dorste ther endure.[33]
>
> The letter said the Queen had been delivered,
> But of some horrible fiend or creature lured
> From Hell itself, and that the castle shivered
> At sight of it, it could not be endured.[34]

Like the Sultan of Syria and his followers, Custance's newborn son is both idealized Christian martyr and monstrous Other. To Custance and those loyal to her, Maurice is described as the ideal heir awaited by Alla; at the same time, he is re-invented by his own grandmother as a demon child. These competing narratives about Maurice result in his playing two radically different roles: a divinely sanctioned Christian offspring and the terrifying product of religious miscegenation. Just as in the Syrian episode, we are presented with a blurring of distinctions, the Other merging into the familiar and vice versa.

This blurring effect, one that makes it hard to determine the alien from the familiar, is especially potent in the Northumbrian episode, in which Custance herself is both foreign and not. Where Custance clearly stood for the familiarity of the Christian world in the Syrian episode, such is not as clearly the case in Northumbria.[35] As with Thomas's mother of legend, we are constantly reminded of Custance's difference, inscribed as it is in her language.[36] Custance's language was not an issue in Syria, suggesting the intriguing possibility that Custance may actually have had more in common with the Sultan than with Alla. Christian though she might be, Custance remains an Easterner, her inability to communicate with the Northumbrians lending some unexpected credence to her characterization by Donegild as "strange."[37] Difference thus becomes increasingly difficult to identify and to distinguish in *The Man of Law's Tale*. If the narrative opens with

---

dismisses this part of the narrative since Custance's child is, in fact, the opposite of monstrous. However, it seems to me important that Donegild creates such a vivid image of Custance's monstrous child, one that seems to rival—if not even eclipse—the real, healthy baby borne by Custance at this point in the narrative.

[33] *The Man of Law's Tale*, lines 750–54.

[34] Chaucer, *The Canterbury Tales*, 161.

[35] By contrast, some scholars have argued the opposite position, namely that Northumbrians are presented as Other in *The Man of Law's Tale*. Kathryn Lynch, for example, claims that: "Although the Northumbrians are native Englanders—and even it turns out harbor conquered Christians in their midst—they are quite provocatively 'orientalized.' The Muslim implications of the King's name—'Alla'—cannot have been lost on Chaucer, or for that matter on his sources. But even compared to these sources, Northumberland seems a place more foreign and strange." Lynch, "Storytelling, Exchange, and Constancy," 417.

[36] Mills, "Invisible Translation," 126.

[37] *The Man of Law's Tale*, line 700.

a clear "us-them" dichotomy, it soon becomes much more difficult to label the Other, first when the Sultaness kills her newly baptized son, then, even more poignantly, when Custance lands on the shores of Northumbria and becomes the Eastern Other.

The Man of Law's Tale does not merely point to unease and discomfort in regards to conversion, but also questions the necessity and usefulness of trying to convert the heathen.[38] This approach to conversion is linked in part to Custance's passivity in Chaucer's version of the narrative. Where Nicholas Trivet and John Gower depict their heroine as actively and enthusiastically engaging in missionary activity, Chaucer's character resists her divine mission from the very first. Unlike the Constance character in the tales of Trivet and Gower, Custance does not convert the Syrian merchants whose report to their Sultan serves as the catalyst to his doomed attempt to convert. Chaucer's merchants do see Custance, but the exchange that is dominated by the emperor's daughter in the versions of the tale by Trivet and Gower never occurs in *The Man of Law's Tale*. The Sultan's love of Custance is based primarily on indirect sources, ones that conventionally privilege her beauty and virtue:

> "In hire is heigh beautee withoute pride,
> Yowthe, withoute grenehede or folye;
> To alle hire werkes vertu is hir gyde;
> Humblesse hath slayn in hire al tirannye.
> She is mirour of alle curteisye;
> Hir herte is verray chambre of hoolynesse,
> Hir hand, ministre of fredam for almesse."[39]

> "Peerless in beauty, yet untouched by pride,
> Young, but untainted by frivolity,
> In all her dealings goodness is her guide,
> And humbleness has vanquished tyranny.
> She is the mirror of all courtesy,
> Her heart the very chamber of holiness,
> Her hand the minister to all distress."[40]

The emphasis on the heroine's agency in *The Anglo-Norman Chronicles* and the *Confessio Amantis* is thus transformed in the hands of Chaucer and his Man of Law into a generic romance trope, the Sultan falling in love with Custance from afar simply by hearing about her beauty and goodness.

Throughout the rest of *The Man of Law's Tale*, Custance's agency is reduced to a minimum, this especially in regards to the character's missionary activity. Except for demurely obeying her father's command, Chaucer's Custance does nothing to convert the Syrian prince. Once in Northumbria, she plays no active role in Alla's conversion, which

---

[38] In "*The Man of Law's Tale* and Crusade," Siobhain Bly Calkin argues that Chaucer uses *The Man of Law's Tale* both to examine contemporary arguments about crusading and to assess the value of "marriage, proselytizing, trade, and money as tools that further crusading goals." Calkin, "*The Man of Law's Tale* and Crusade," 2–3.

[39] *The Man of Law's Tale*, lines 162–68.

[40] Chaucer, *The Canterbury Tales*, 144.

is merely described as the result of "Custances mediacioun" ([Constance's] mediation).[41] As noted above, even her marriage is accomplished through Jesus's direct intervention.[42] Her conscious missionary activity consists solely of the conversion of Hermengild when she first washes up on the shores of Northumbria. In Chauncey Wood's words:

> While she is an active preacher of God's word in Trivet's version of the story, she is virtually without volition in the Man of Law's redaction. She has ceased to be a person who exerts influence on other people, and has been changed into an object to be moved about by forces over which she has no control and little understanding.[43]

Here, it is interesting to note that Custance's speech to her parents on the eve of her departure from Rome not only differentiates Custance from the manifestations of the Constance character fashioned by Trivet and Gower but also recalls the speech addressed by the princess of Tars to her parents when the Sultan of Damascus declares war against their kingdom out of a desire for the princess's hand.[44] Although initially less active than the characters of Trivet and Gower, the princess of Tars uses her words to convince her parents to facilitate her marriage to the Sultan, thereby saving her people from destruction. Like the Constance characters fashioned by Trivet and Gower, the princess takes action into her own hands and uses language to facilitate peace and, ultimately, the conversion of the Other. Thus, not only is conversion fraught with anxiety and suspicion in *The Man of Law's Tale*, but the saintly figure at the heart of the narrative also engages in as little missionary activity as possible.

If active missionary work appears far less appealing in *The Man of Law's Tale* than it does in *The King of Tars* and the versions of the Constance tale composed by Nicholas Trivet and John Gower, conversion also does not seem to reap the same benefits for those who choose to embrace Christianity in the imaginary world of Chaucer's tale. The Sultan of Syria pays for his conversion with his life. In Northumbria, where Custance's passive missionary activity meets with much greater success, the benefits of adopting Christianity remain slim. Not only does Alla's conversion lead to his murder of Donegild, but it also costs him his heir, for Maurice, the one and only child born to Alla and Custance, becomes the Roman Emperor's rather than Alla's heir.[45] In Trivet's version, the designation of Maurice as the emperor's heir causes no dynastic disruption: Alla has an older son, Edwin, whom he leaves in charge of Northumberland when he leaves for Rome.[46] Presumably, Edwin will succeed as king of Northumbria at the death of Alla and the defection of Maurice.[47] By contrast, Chaucer makes no mention of Alla having any

---

41 *The Man of Law's Tale*, line 684; Chaucer, *The Canterbury Tales*, 159.
42 *The Man of Law's Tale*, lines 690–93.
43 Chauncey Wood, "Chaucer's Man of Law as Interpreter," *Traditio* 23 (1967): 149–90 at 186.
44 *The Man of Law's Tale*, lines 274–87.
45 *The Man of Law's Tale*, lines 1121–22.
46 Margaret Schlauch, "*The Man of Law's Tale*," in *Sources and Analogues of Chaucer's Canterbury Tales*, ed. W. F. Bryan and Germaine Dempster (Chicago: University of Chicago Press, 1941), 178.
47 In "'To Aleppo Gone': From the North Sea to Syria in Chaucer's *Man of Law's Tale* and Shakespeare's *Macbeth*," Nicholas Birns notes that Edwin was indeed the son of Aella of Deira, the

heirs beyond Maurice, and we are left to wonder if strife and chaos follow upon Alla's death as a result of his marriage to Custance.

The ending of *The Man of Law's Tale* echoes its opening in its ambiguous approach to conversion. While the versions of the story composed by Trivet and Gower follows each of the main characters, Alla, the emperor, and Custance, to the end of their lives—Trivet is especially precise in allotting specific amounts of time between each character's passing: Alla dies nine months after returning to England, the emperor six months later, and Constance a year after that—Chaucer emphasizes only the passing of Alla, who dies exactly one year after his reunion with Custance in *The Man of Law's Tale*.[48] Once Alla has died, Custance returns home to her father and friends:

> To Rome is come this hooly creature,
> And fyndeth hire freendes hoole and sounde;
> Now is she scaped al hire aventure.
> And whan that she hir fader hath yfounde,
> Doun on hir knees falleth she to grounde;
> Wepynge for tendrenesse in herte blithe,
> She heryeth God an hundred thousand sithe.
>
> In vertu and in hooly almus-dede
> They lyven alle, and nevere asonder wende;
> Til deeth departeth hem, this lyf they lede.[49]
>
> To Rome she came, this holy soul, at last,
> And found her friends again at home and well;
> All her adventures now were safely past;
> She found her father in the citadel
> And weeping tears of tenderness she fell
> Joyfully on her knees, pouring her praises
> In thanks to God, a thousand eager phrases.
>
> And so they lived in virtue and the giving
> Of holy alms, never again to wend
> Until by death divided from the living;[50]

As a result of this change in tone, the tale ends on a very different note. As Chauncey Wood puts it:

> At the end of the story, Custance's blithe heart, her safe and sound friends, her end to adventure and her future life without separation from her father all combine to paint for us an unmistakably happy picture, which is in marked contrast to the original in which it is explicitly stated that Custance's father dies six months after Alla, and she herself one year after that. Chaucer has made a change in tone here that does violence to the original and to the "interpretation" of this world maintained by the Man of Law...Thus the story of Custance, which in Trivet's version terminates with the deaths of all and sundry con-

---

historical figure upon which King Alla is based, and that he—unlike the historical Aella—converted to Christianity. Birns, "'To Aleppo Gone,'" 368.

48 *The Man of Law's Tale*, lines 1143–44.
49 *The Man of Law's Tale*, lines 1149–58.
50 Chaucer, *The Canterbury Tales*, 172.

cerned, here is brought to a close on an incongruously happy note, and is followed in the text by the Man of Law's remarkable invocation of Christ as the bringer of good Fortune.[51]

The happy ending given Custance in *The Man of Law's Tale* impacts the narrative's message about conversion and missionary work. Whereas Trivet and Gower celebrate Custance's return to God once her missionary work is complete, Chaucer's Man of Law suggests that Custance's reward for her suffering and her conversion of Northumbria takes the shape of Alla's death and her return to the home she never wanted to leave. Instead of granting Custance a finite amount of time in Rome with her father, Chaucer sets no limits on the remainder of Custance's time in Rome with the emperor. The heroine's reward has thus shifted from being granted admission to the heavenly realm to being permitted to return to her earthly home. This shift is significant, for it betrays a certain indifference—perhaps even distaste—for the kind of missionary activity to which conversion of the Other is central. Custance's mission, like that of the Constance of Trivet and Gower, may be to convert Northumbria to Christianity but, unlike these other versions of the character, she possesses no enthusiasm for it. What she really longs for from the moment her father betroths her to the Sultan of Syria is simply to return home.

Conversion in *The Man of Law's Tale* is a messy, unrewarding business. As shown by the ambiguous identity of the newly converted Sultan of Syria—and even by Maurice and Custance herself—the narrative blurs the lines between non-Christian and Christian, foreign and familiar, making it increasingly difficult to distinguish one from the other as the tale unfolds. When conversion does take place, it is either not successful—in the case of Custance's first marriage to the Sultan of Syria—or only partially successful—in Northumbria, Custance fails at converting Donegild. And when all ends well, the reward is not the heavenly kingdom but a return to the home the heroine had to leave to embark on her mission of conversion. In the end, Custance's reward lies in her no longer having to sail to foreign shores to convert the Other to Christianity. The ultimate compensation for missionary activity, the Man of Law implies, lies in no longer having to concern oneself with missionary activity.

Conclusions

The Becket legend both introduces anxieties about the conversion of the Other while also seeking to reassure its audience about such fears. It is for this reason that the legend cannot end with the saint's conception, proving instead that the non-Christian princess *does* assimilate into English society. Having confronted its original audience with the terrifying prospect of the invasion of English soil by the Other—the princess's difference on evidence in her inability to speak English or be understood by London burghers— all doubt as to the place of Thomas Becket's mother in her new Christian community must be eliminated.

The Man of Law's Tale, a story that likewise focuses on a woman guided across the ocean to the shores of England by God, deals with conversion and anxiety about con-

---

[51] Wood, "Chaucer's Man of Law as Interpreter," 188.

version very differently from the Becket legend. Where the legend ultimately resolves lingering doubts and concerns about Thomas's mother, *The Man of Law's Tale* amplifies any anxiety its audience might harbor about the conversion of the Other, representing missionary work as hazardous, threatening, confusing, and, in the long run, unrewarding. The contrast between the two narratives is important: the Becket legend treats conversion with ambiguity whereas *The Man of Law's Tale* blurs the distinction between the familiar and the Other. Like many earlier medieval texts, the Becket legend initially privileges religious difference prior to emphasizing the role of other, non-religious markers of difference. Eventually, the legend concludes that non-religious difference can be overcome and that the new convert can, in time, assimilate fully into his or her new community. By contrast, *The Man of Law's Tale* at first presents difference as easily distinguishable from the familiar only for that boundary to become increasingly difficult to delineate. In the end, difference pervades every aspect of *The Man of Law's Tale*, marking even Custance, the heroine, and her son, the future emperor of Rome. If the Other becomes familiar in the Becket legend, the opposite takes place in *The Man of Law's Tale*, and the seemingly familiar becomes "strange."

In considering the ways in which *The Man of Law's Tale* departs from the earlier legend, it is essential to remember that the two are intricately connected, the Becket legend having served as a secondary source in the composition of *The Man of Law's Tale*. As such, Chaucer's diverging approach to conversion, an issue central to both narratives, appears even more significant.

Chapter 4

THE MAN OF LAW'S TALE IN CONTEXT

Of course, there exist several important differences between narratives such as the Becket legend, *The King of Tars*, and *Bevis of Hampton* and *The Man of Law's Tale*, not the least of which lies in that Chaucer's narrative belongs to a larger work of tremendous complexity, *The Canterbury Tales*. As such, we cannot draw any deeper conclusions about the treatment of conversion in *The Man of Law's Tale* without addressing the place and function of the tale and its teller within the larger scope of *The Canterbury Tales*. Here, it is not only necessary to examine the role of *The Man of Law's Tale* in *The Canterbury Tales*, but also to interrogate the Man of Law and to evaluate both his portrait in *The General Prologue* and his relationship to the story he chooses to tell on the way to Canterbury and to the shrine of Thomas Becket. These questions have been the subject of long discussions for over a century; in the following pages, I will only raise them to further elucidate Chaucer's approach to the conversion of the Other, trying to gage the extent to which the disinterest towards the process of conversion noted in the previous chapter belongs to Chaucer or simply to the Man of Law. Where a simple reading of narratives such as the Becket legend and *Bevis of Hampton* can lead us to understand the story's underlying message about baptism and conversion, this is not the case with *The Man of Law's Tale*. Having assessed the tale's ambiguous and ultimately negative approach to conversion, we must now ask whether the tale's apparent distaste for conversion constitutes yet another facet of the character fabricated by Chaucer or whether these views in fact align themselves with the poet's own understanding of the role of conversion in interacting with the Muslim Other in England in the late fourteenth century.

In undertaking such an analysis of *The Man of Law's Tale* and its teller and trying to ascertain the place and function of both in Chaucer's *Canterbury Tales*, I will set aside the Becket legend for a while, focusing instead on the relationship between the Man of Law and other pilgrims. Yet, it is important to remember that the Becket legend and *The Man of Law's Tale* both belong to the genre of popular devotional literature. In fact, it is the influence of the Becket legend that allows *The Man of Law's Tale* to convey the devotional message central to grasping the tale's wider significance in the *Tales*. The Becket legend may appear absent from the discussion that follows, but, in actuality, it remains necessary to approaching the tale in its wider context.

The Man of Law's Tale and the Man of Law: The Tale and Its Teller

To begin, we must return to that vexed question, one that has plagued Chaucerians and their reading of *The Canterbury Tales* for centuries, namely the relationship between teller and tale. Who is the Man of Law and is there anything in his portrait that would suggest the pessimistic approach to conversion outlined in the previous chapter? His initial portrayal in *The General Prologue* is mostly positive:

CHAPTER 4

> A Sergeant of the Lawe, war and wys,
> That often hadde been at the Parvys,
> Ther was also, ful riche of excellence.
> Discreet he was and of greet reverence—
> He semed swich, his wordes weren so wise.
> Justice he was ful often in assise,
> By patente and by pleyn commissioun.
> For his science, and for his heigh renoun,
> Of fees and robes hadde he many oon.
> So greet a purchasour was nowher noon:
> Al was fee symple to hym in effect;
> His purchasyng myghte nat been infect.
> Nowher so bisy a man as he ther nas,
> And yet he semed bisier than he was.
> In termes hadde he caas and doomes alle
> That from the tyme of kyng William were falle.
> Therto he koude endite and make a thyng,
> Ther koude no wight pynche at his writyng;
> And every statut koude he pleyn by rote.
> He rood but hoomly in a medlee cote,
> Girt with a ceint of silk, with barres smale;
> Of his array telle I no lenger tale.[1]

> A Serjeant at the Law who paid his calls,
> Wary and wise, for clients at St Paul's
> There also was, of noted excellence.
> Discreet he was, a man to reverence,
> Or so he seemed, his sayings were so wise.
> He often had been Justice of Assize
> By letters patent, and in full commission.
> His fame and learning and his high position
> Had won him many a robe and many a fee.
> There was no such conveyancer as he;
> All was fee-simple to his strong digestion,
> Not one conveyance could be called in question.
> Nowhere there was so busy a man as he;
> But was less busy than he seemed to be.
> He knew of every judgement, case and crime
> Recorded, ever since King William's time.
> He could dictate defences or draft deeds;
> No one could pinch a comma from his screeds,
> And he knew every statute off by rote.
> He wore a homely parti-coloured coat
> Girt with a silken belt of pin-stripe stuff;
> Of his appearance I have said enough.[2]

The Man of Law is depicted as articulate, discreet, well-learned in his profession, and honoured by his peers. Being a man of law makes him a "new man," to use Anne

---

1 *The General Prologue*, lines 309–30.
2 Chaucer, *The Canterbury Tales*, 27–28.

Middleton's term, but his portrait otherwise marks him as superior in education, character, and virtue to most of his fellow pilgrims.[3]

The only hint that there might be another, less appealing side to the Man of Law occurs at line 322, when Chaucer the narrator tells us that "he semed bisier than he was."[4] Here, Chaucer suggests that the Man of Law's polished appearance might be a carefully constructed illusion. The use of the word "semed," one already employed earlier in the portrait—"He semed swich" at line 313—further directs our attention to the possibility that fabrication and pretense play important roles in this pilgrim's presentation of himself to the world. In this, he is not alone, for the Merchant is also depicted positively as a successful "new man" only for that impression to be reversed by the allusion to his debt two thirds into his own portrait.[5] The portrait of the Man of Law thus gives us a few important pieces of information about this character. Like most of the pilgrims headed towards Thomas's shrine at Canterbury, he is not a "gentil." He is, however, a prominent city burgher. Yet, there lies a hint of untrustworthiness in the Man of Law's introduction, one that makes us question whether the lawyer truly excels at his profession or whether he merely plays the part of a successful man of law. Finally, I would argue that the similarity between the portrait of the Man of Law and that of the Merchant is not fortuitous and that Chaucer here points to a connection between the Man of Law and merchants, a point to which I will return later.

The impression given of the Man of Law in his introductory portrait in *The General Prologue* is reinforced in the exchange between the Host and the Man of Law that immediately precedes *The Man of Law's Prologue*. The Man of Law's first words emphasize his profession, the seven lines he spends asserting to the Host that he means to keep his vow to tell a story evidence of his inability to forget the law even while taking part in a game.[6] If anything, the officiousness with which he approaches the storytelling competition lends him the air of a bore, someone so entranced by the letter of the law that he cannot see beyond it.

This initial portrayal of the Man of Law is rendered more ambiguous a little later on, and we are once again made aware that appearances can be deceiving. Having introduced some of Chaucer's earlier works—for example, *The Legend of Good Women*—the Man of Law highlights a handful of classical female characters.[7] In this passage, he shows a talent for describing narratives both concisely and graphically so as to allow his audience to visualize crucial episodes, particularly those of a horrific and dramatic nature. For instance, his summary of the Medea legend includes the line, "thy litel children hangynge by the hals" (her little children hanging by the neck), leaving the Man of

---

3 Anne Middleton, "Chaucer's 'New Men' and the Good of Literature in the *Canterbury Tales*," in *Literature and Society*, edited by Edward W. Said (Baltimore: Johns Hopkins University Press, 1980), 15–56, as cited in Lavezzo, "Beyond Rome," 178.

4 As mentioned by A. C. Spearing in "Narrative Voice: The Case of Chaucer's *Man of Law's Tale*." Spearing, "Narrative Voice," 719.

5 *The General Prologue*, line 280.

6 *The Man of Law's Prologue*, lines 39–45.

7 *The Man of Law's Prologue*, lines 62–76.

Law's audience with a searing image of Medea's horrifying crime of infanticide.[8] Like the Prioress, the Man of Law shows a predilection for melodrama and pathos.[9]

The Man of Law's prurient interest in victimized innocence stands out even more clearly in the lines that follow his summary of the story of Medea. Immediately upon stressing that he refuses to speak of incestuous love, such as that of Canace and her brother, the Man of Law provides another concise, yet highly visual summary of King Antiochus's rape of his daughter.[10] Just as he earlier used the word "hals" to convey a clear image of Medea's dead children, so now does the Man of Law add a detail that makes the incestuous rape especially vivid:

> How that the cursed kyng Antiochus
> Birafte his doghter of hir maydenhede,
> That is so horrible a tale for to rede,
> Whan he hir threw upon the pavement.[11]

> How King Antiochus in mad desire
> Bereft his daughter of her maidenhead.
> The tale's too horrible, it can't be read.
> He flung her on the pavement for his wooing![12]

The reference to the paved floor upon which the king throws his daughter before raping her again heightens the pathos and drama of the story while ensuring that the Man of Law's audience can visualize the scene as clearly as possible. Where his earlier description of Medea's children might have made his fellow pilgrims uncomfortable—both because of the disturbing image itself and because of the obvious relish with which he imparts it to them—the details the Man of Law provides about the rape of Antiochus's daughter now also show him to be a liar. He may tell his companions that he does not want to indulge in narratives of incest, but the fact that he takes the time and effort to describe Antiochus's assault on his own daughter so vividly tells quite a different story. At this point in the opening exchange between Harry Bailly and the Man of Law, the latter has thus not only reinforced the impression that there is more to the character than initially meets the eye but he has also done so in the most unsettling way possible.[13]

---

8 *The Man of Law's Prologue*, line 73; Chaucer, *The Canterbury Tales*, 141.

9 The adjective "litel"—privileged by the Prioress in her own graphically violent tale—plays an important role in conveying the graphic scene of Medea's murdered children in this very brief passage. Again like the Prioress, the Man of Law appears to focus particularly on children in his brief dramatization of classical tragedies.

10 *The Man of Law's Prologue*, lines 78–79 and lines 81–85.

11 *The Man of Law's Prologue*, lines 82–85.

12 Chaucer, *The Canterbury Tales*, 141.

13 At line 96 of *The Man of Law's Prologue*, the Man of Law announces that he will tell his tale in prose rather than verse, a statement that—since *The Man of Law's Tale* is in fact told in rhyme—has led scholars to debate whether Chaucer did intend the Man of Law to tell the story of Constance. According to Carleton Brown, for example: "Chaucer's earlier arrangement seems to have been: the General Prologue (11. 1–826), followed by the Man of Law's head-link with the Tale of Melibeus, followed in turn (according to the large majority of MSS) by the Squire's Tale and the Franklin's. From this point the existing MSS show such complications in their arrangement that it is not

In the brief prologue to *The Man of Law's Tale* that follows, the Man of Law devotes three of five stanzas to the horrors of poverty, the theme as he sees it of his tale. According to Michael Calabrese, the Man of Law here reveals his lack of education and understanding, for he alludes to and seeks to illustrate Pope Innocent III's treatise *De miseria*, which deplores poverty and wealth equally.[14] Yet, the Man of Law parrots Innocent's words about poverty and indigence while extolling, rather than condemning, wealth.

It is, in fact, while speaking about the ills of poverty that the Man of Law evokes merchants for the first time, and the merchant class features prominently in the last two stanzas of *The Man of Law's Prologue*. Merchants, to the Man of Law, do not have to worry about poverty: They represent wealth and ease. the Man of Law's remarks about the merchant class, ones included in his short prologue both because the Man of Law sees trade as the antithesis to poverty but also, and perhaps more importantly, because he owes his tale to merchants in his acquaintance, further illustrate that the Man of Law's knowledge and understanding, like his appearance, are not quite what they seem. His blithe assertion that merchants do not know want and poverty is jarring in its naivete, coming, as it does, after the portrait of the Merchant, a man whom we know to be in debt. Like the Merchant, the Man of Law appears more professional and successful than he might truly be, but the Merchant's improvidence also points to the Man of Law's inability to understand the meaning of his own tale.

A portrait of the Man of Law emerges in his portrait in *The General Prologue* as well as in the exchange with Harry Bailly and his own brief prologue to his tale, one that reveals a man whose ambitions far exceed his knowledge and understanding. Through his retelling of the story of Constance, the Man of Law seeks to engage in the debate about Fate and Free Will initiated by the Knight while also providing the crusading tale the other pilgrims expected but did not receive from the Knight. As such, the Man of Law utilizes the storytelling competition both to insinuate himself amongst the "gentils" and to attempt to surpass the Knight, the paragon chosen to tell the first tale due to his status and reputation. With *The Man of Law's Tale*, the Man of Law provides a Christian response to the question about Fate and Free Will first posed by the Knight while also giving his tale the crusading aura missing from the Knight's own classical narrative. In fact, Kathy Lavezzo has argued that the Man of Law sets his tale in not one but all of the locations identified by the storytellers of the First Fragment, "while the Knight grandly transports his auditors to Athens, and the Miller, Reeve, and Cook modestly remain within the confines of England, the Man of Law straddles the line between the world's

---

possible to trace Chaucer's plan with any certainty." (Carleton Brown, "The Man of Law's Head-Link and the Prologue of *The Canterbury Tales*," *Studies in Philology*, 34, no. 1 (1937): 33.

A. C. Spearing, by contrast, refutes this theory, arguing that: "To attribute the tale in which such probing questions are asked to the blindness and errors of the Man of Law is to refuse to plumb the metaphysical depths that Chaucer was prepared to contemplate. I hope it has emerged from this study that to read the *Man of Law's Tale* as spoken in the voice of a fictional narrator is usually to avoid reading it all." (Spearing, "Narrative Voice," 742).

14 Michael Calabrese, "*The Man of Law's Tale* as a Keystone to *The Canterbury Tales*," in *Approaches to Teaching Chaucer's Canterbury Tales*, ed. Peter W. Travis and Frank Grady (New York: Modern Language Association of America, 2014), 85.

English edge and its classical centers."[15] Here again, the Man of Law attempts to outdo his predecessors, focusing on England *and* the classical world.

Despite his ambitious aspirations, the Man of Law ultimately fails to succeed in fashioning a tale that can truly rival the aesthetic and narrative value of *The Knight's Tale*. Not only does *The Man of Law's Tale* lack the beauty and intricacy of the earlier tales, but the manner in which the Man of Law deals with conversion and missionary activity further weakens his message about divine Providence and the importance of proselytizing. Unlike Warner, I would further argue that *The Man of Law's Tale* is a narrative about crusading only in the most superficial of ways, its message and theme belying the differentiation between English and Syrian necessary to preaching crusade ideology. The Man of Law's lack of true understanding—of divine Providence, of learned clerical treatises such as the *De miseria*, of the superiority of the heavenly realm over the material one—leads him to create a passive heroine who prefers to act as a vessel of God's divine will rather than actively engage in missionary work and whose reward comes in the form of returning home upon the completion of her divine mission. While contending that he belongs with master storytellers such as the Knight, the Man of Law shows his lack of true knowledge and his simple, superstitious approach to religion.

Perhaps the connection drawn between the Man of Law and the merchant class, both through the similarity of his portrait in *The General Prologue* to that of the Merchant and to his own acknowledgment that his tale was given him by merchants, informs his failure to grasp the wider spiritual meaning of his tale. Through the lens of a merchant's eye, there is no need for Custance to seek out foreigners and the natives of strange lands to convert them to Christianity. Conversion ought not to be a merchant's primary goal; in fact, from a merchant's perspective, it makes far more sense for Custance to drift from one shore to another without embroiling herself in the lives of the peoples she meets than for her to attempt to convert them. And, of course, a merchant would reward Custance by returning her to her home. The perplexing ending that diminishes the value of missionary activity otherwise extolled in the tale makes perfect sense from a merchant's perspective. After all, can we not imagine fourteenth-century merchants dreading the dangers of sea voyage and fantasizing about coming home and never having to leave it again? Thus, *The Man of Law's Tale*, raised to thunderous heights by the pilgrim's ambitious desire to be seen as an equal and a rival to the Knight and other "gentils," fails because his vision remains that of a burgher with a far greater affinity for merchants and other "new men" than any noble lord.

If gaining a better understanding of the Man of Law as a character and a storyteller allows us greater insight into the tale and the ways in which it diverges from Chaucer's primary sources, it still does not tell us whether the Man of Law's vision of conversion also belongs to Chaucer or not. In order to find an answer to this question, we must first establish the place of *The Man of Law's Tale* in *The Canterbury Tales* as a whole.

---

15 Lavezzo, "Beyond Rome," 178.

The Man of Law's Tale within the Larger Context of The Canterbury Tales

To assess the place of *The Man of Law's Tale* in *The Canterbury Tales* constitutes no small feat. There exist many different ways in which to approach the Man of Law and his tale, from his engagement and response to the First Fragment to his intriguing connection with the Squire in a significant number of manuscripts.[16] In dealing with the question of the role of *The Man of Law's Tale* in Chaucer's magnum opus, however, I will guide us on a less obvious path. Rather than look at the tales that come before *The Man of Law's Tale* and the pilgrims the Man of Law addresses directly, particularly the Knight, I would like to investigate the exchange between the Host, the Man of Law, and the Parson at the *end* of *The Man of Law's Tale* so as to discuss the possible relationship between *The Man of Law's Tale* and the Parson and his own, concluding tale.

Chaucer couples *The Man of Law's Tale* with *The Parson's Tale* by giving both their tellers narratives that fit broadly within the genre of popular devotional literature—something that can also be said for the Becket legend—and by focusing on the Parson in *The Epilogue of the Man of Law's Tale*, also known as the *Endlink*. Undoubtedly, the Man of Law does not possess much in common with the Parson, and their narratives likewise differ strikingly from each other. The Man of Law, a man concerned with the spiritual but still very much rooted in this world, tells the story of a saint who also becomes a wife and a mother. In contrast, the Parson, whose life revolves solely around his parishioners, dismisses all worldly elements from his own story, a sermon that denounces the fictional. The Parson and his tale stand diametrically opposed to the Man of Law and his retelling of the Constance narrative. Yet, one might also perceive these two very different tales to be complementing each other. The Man of Law shifts the pilgrims' attention to spiritual matters and, indirectly, to the Parson. The Parson may not be ready to speak directly after the Man of Law but, perhaps, the Parson *could* not speak without the earlier interference of the Man of Law.

Before launching into a discussion of *The Man of Law's Tale* and *The Parson's Tale* as two examples of popular devotional literature, I would like to begin by distinguishing between two terms: "religion" and "religiosity." As R. N. Swanson notes in *Religion and Devotion in Europe, c. 1215–c. 1515*:

> In an important contribution, Gavin Langmuir has recently proposed a distinction between "religion", the system of beliefs prescribed by the ecclesiastical authorities and "religiosity", the format in which individuals construct a spiritually satisfying enactment of that religion.[17]

Medieval "religiosity," according to Langmuir and Swanson, did not necessarily always align itself perfectly with "religion" or the practices and ideologies of the church. It is on "religiosity" or popular devotion, as I will refer to it, and its expression in *The Canterbury*

---

[16] *The Squire's Tale* follows *The Man of Law's Tale* in thirty-three manuscripts of *The Canterbury Tales*. Lynch, "Storytelling, Exchange, and Constancy," 419.

[17] R. N. Swanson, *Religion and Devotion in Europe, c. 1215–c. 1515* (Cambridge: Cambridge University Press, 1995), 8.

Tales—particularly in *The Man of Law's Tale* and *The Parson's Tale*—that I will focus in the next few pages.

According to the distinction made by Langmuir and Swanson, both *The Man of Law's Tale* and *The Parson's Tale* belong to the broad genre of popular devotional literature or "religiosity." In the case of *The Man of Law's Tale*, the very romance elements that distinguish the tale from more conventional saints' lives point to the popular devotional nature of the narrative.[18] As for *The Parson's Tale*, it exemplifies "religiosity" or popular devotional literature even more clearly, accomplishing precisely what such popular works were expected to.[19] In his discussion of popular access to the faith, Swanson specifically refers to *The Parson's Tale* as a type of popular devotional guide, "confessional manuals which catalogued sins could still find lay audiences: the discussion of sin and its remedies in Chaucer's *Parson's Tale* is derived from just such compilations."[20] Although outwardly divergent, both of Chaucer's tales thus fit squarely in the category of religiosity as opposed to official, church-sanctioned religious literature.

That the Man of Law chooses to tell a narrative belonging to the genre of popular devotional literature immediately after the First Fragment carries great significance since *The Man of Law's Tale* constitutes the first overtly religious tale in the collection. As many have argued, the tale seems to mark a new beginning, one that re-orients the pilgrims towards the ideal of pilgrimage generally and Canterbury more specifically.[21] By drawing on the Becket legend, the Man of Law tries not only to direct his companions' attention to loftier spiritual themes, but also to the saint himself.[22]

In addition to belonging to the same broad genre, the link between *The Man of Law's Tale* and *The Parson's Tale* is made even more explicit in thirty-five of the remaining manuscripts of *The Canterbury Tales*, in which *The Man of Law's Tale* is followed by *The Epilogue of the Man of Law's Tale* or *Endlink*.[23] In this piece, the Host calls on the Parson to tell the next tale:

> Owre Hoost upon his stiropes stood anoon,
> And seyde, "Goode men, herkeneth everych on!

---

18 *Mirk's Festial*, a late medieval compilation of sermons, includes the Becket legend. Swanson, however, argues that such sermons "acquire literary characteristics and functions, and are perhaps unrepresentative of the reality of contemporary sermonising." Swanson, *Religion and Devotion*, 64. *The Man of Law's Tale*, likewise, can be viewed as a sermon with "literary characteristics and functions" while *The Parson's Tale* lies closer to "the reality of contemporary sermonising."

19 Swanson, *Religion and Devotion in Europe*, 27.

20 Swanson, *Religion and Devotion in Europe*, 59.

21 Susan Schibanoff cites three prominent Chaucerians, Derek Pearsall, Helen Cooper, and V. A. Kolve, that made this claim at the opening of her piece. Other critics, such as Kevin J. Harty and R. A. Shoaf, have likewise noted this aspect of *The Man of Law's Tale*. Schibanoff, "Worlds Apart," 59–60; Harty, "The Tale and Its Teller," 361; and R. A. Shoaf, "'Unwemmed Custance': Circulation, Property, and Incest in *The Man of Law's Tale*," *Exemplaria*, 2, no. 1 (March 1990): 298.

22 As mentioned earlier, some scholars have argued that Chaucer originally intended to give the Man of Law *The Tale of Melibee*. For more on the Man of Law and *The Tale of Melibee*, see Brown, "The Man of Law's Head-Link," 33.

23 Lynch, "Storytelling, Exchange, and Constancy," 419.

> This was a thrifty tale for the nones!
> Sire Parisshe Prest," quod he, "for Goddes bones,
> Telle us a tale, as was thi forward yore.
> I se wel that ye lerned men in lore
> Can moche good, by Goddes dignitee!"[24]

> Our Host, after the Man of Law had done
> Rose in his stirrups. "Listen, everyone,
> Good value, that," he said, "to say the least,
> A thrifty tale, God's bones, Sir Parish Priest,
> Tell us a tale! You promised it before.
> You learned men are full of ancient lore,
> God's dignity! You know a lot, I see."[25]

The Parson responds by dismissing the Host. The Host then replies in kind by denouncing the Parson as a "Lollere" (Lollard).[26]

There exist two important aspects to the failed transition from the Man of Law to the Parson, the first of which lies in the association made by the Host between the two pilgrims and their stories. The Host clearly recognizes the devotional nature of *The Man of Law's Tale* and feels that the retelling of the story of Constance provides an adequate prelude to a tale composed by the Parson. To the Host, *The Man of Law's Tale* is religious enough to lead into *The Parson's Tale*.

The Parson, however, disagrees. To the Parson, *The Man of Law's Tale* is still far too worldly. The one truly dedicated religious individual on the pilgrimage, the Parson criticizes the Host's language, perhaps because he also rejects the Host's facile assumption that his tale will bear any resemblance to that of the Man of Law.[27] Although his tale, like *The Man of Law's Tale*, belongs to the genre of popular devotional literature, it requires a level of commitment to the spiritual not yet to be found amongst the Canterbury pilgrims.

The Host reacts to the Parson's criticism with anger:

> Oure Host answerde, "O Jankin, be ye there?
> I smelle a Lollere in the wynd!" quod he.
> "Now! goode men," quod oure Hoste, "herkeneth me;
> Abydeth, for Goddes digne passioun,
> For we schal han a predicacioun;
> This Lollere heer wil prechen us somwhat."[28]

> Our Host retorted, "Ho! Is Johnny there?
> I smell a Lollard in the wind!" said he.
> "Good men," our Host went on, "attend to me;
> Don't run away! By Jesu's noble passion,
> We're in for something done in sermon-fashion.
> This Lollard here would like to preach, that's what."[29]

---

24 *The Epilogue of the Man of Law's Tale*, lines 1163–69.
25 Chaucer, *The Canterbury Tales*, 173.
26 *The Epilogue of the Man of Law's Tale*, lines 1173 and 1177; Chaucer, *The Canterbury Tales*, 173.
27 *The Epilogue of the Man of Law's Tale*, lines 1170–71.
28 *The Epilogue of the Man of Law's Tale*, lines 1172–77.
29 Chaucer, *The Canterbury Tales*, 173.

The Host's words suggest that he expects the Parson to tell a work of fiction perhaps not unlike *The Man of Law's Tale* in its interweaving of romance, adventure, and hagiography. What the Host does not anticipate is for the Parson to tell a sermon, shedding all of the chaff to leave his audience with nothing but the purest wheat.[30] At this juncture, the connection made between the Man of Law and the Parson by the Host appears fractious at best: the *Endlink* presents the Host as misapprehending the Parson on the premise of his false understanding of and mistaken approach to religion and spirituality. The Host turns from the Man of Law to the Parson out of an ignorant belief that the narrative given the pilgrims by the Man of Law, a story told him by merchants and filled with romance elements, is a spiritual tale. The Parson's emphatic, almost hostile response constitutes his first attempt to correct the Host and the rest of the pilgrims by setting them on the right spiritual path. But *The Man of Law's Tale* is *not* enough, and the Host balks at the Parson's stark words, allowing the pilgrims to revert to more worldly topics prior to returning to the Parson at the very end of the pilgrimage.

Only then, in the final moments of the pilgrimage, do the Host and the rest of the pilgrims open themselves fully to the Parson and his message, the Host and Parson interacting much more fruitfully and successfully than in the *Endlink*. The second exchange between Host and Parson is in many ways similar to the first:

> "Sire preest," quod he, "artow a vicary?
> Or arte a person? Sey sooth, by thy fey!
> Be what thou be, ne breke thou nat oure pley;
> For every man, save thou, hath toold his tale.
> Unbokele and shewe us what is in thy male;
> For trewely, me thynketh by thy cheere
> Thou sholdest knytte up wel a greet mateere.
> Telle us a fable anon, for cokkes bones!"[31]

> "Sir Priest," he said, "are you by chance a vicar?
> Or else the parson? Tell the truth I say;
> Don't spoil our sport though, be you what you may,
> For every man but you has told his tale.
> Unbuckle now and show what's in your bale,
> For honestly, to judge you by your looks,
> You could knit mighty matters out of books.
> So up and tell a story, by cock's bones!"[32]

As in in his initial exchange with the Parson, the Host begins by alluding to the Parson's profession before reminding him of his pledge to partake in the storytelling contest. Harry Bailly then states his belief that the Parson will make a good storyteller and will benefit the rest of the company. On both occasions, the Host also swears, invoking God's bones.

Despite the similar structure of these two exchanges, several subtle, but significant differences emerge between the two passages. Where the Host initially addresses the

---

30 *The Parson's* Prologue, lines 35–36.
31 *The Parson's* Prologue, lines 22–29.
32 Chaucer, *The Canterbury Tales*, 503.

Parson with confidence, labeling him a parish priest and a "lerned" man without further inquiry, he enjoins the Parson to identify himself on his own terms in *The Parson's Prologue*. Likewise, his tone is less assured—almost pleading—when he bids the Parson to contribute a tale to the storytelling competition. And when he does finally revert to swearing, it is with the euphemistic "cokkes bones" rather than "Goddes bones" in an attempt to respect and heed the Parson's earlier condemnation of swearing.[33]

Nor is the Host the only one to have altered his behaviour. The Parson is more than willing to accept the Host's peace offering, ignoring the milder curse and simply laying out the rules according to which he will participate in the storytelling contest.[34] The exchange is courteous and civil and ends—in most manuscripts—on the Host invoking God's grace.[35] The conversation between Host and Parson in *The Parson's Prologue* thus mirrors that in the *Endlink* to *The Man of Law's Tale*. This time, however, the characters' interaction is grounded in mutual respect and collaboration, the secular and religious worlds working together for the greater good.

It might be argued that such similarities do not suggest anything more than a passing connection between the Man of Law, the Parson, and the pilgrims' respective tales. After all, the Parson does *not* give his tale until much later in the collection, and *The Man of Law's Tale* does not solicit a properly spiritual continuation. As the collection has been preserved for us, the sheer physical distance between *The Man of Law's Tale* and *The Parson's Tale* divides the two narratives on the most basic level.

And yet, the Parson can only tell his tale because of the Man of Law and his narrative. *The Man of Law's Tale* reminds pilgrims and audiences alike of the spiritual goal of the pilgrimage, doing so not merely by focusing on the saintly conduct of Custance, but also by echoing the Becket legend and thereby pointing us in the direction of Canterbury. If the tale of the Man of Law is not enough to elevate the pilgrims to a more spiritual understanding of life, it is because of its reliance on romance elements and its deliberate appeal to lay audiences. The Man of Law is too rooted in this world and lacking in any real understanding of the spiritual goals of the pilgrimage. As one might expect of a lawyer, he approaches his pilgrimage as a journey with a tangible, physical goal. Like his tale, the Man of Law's perception of pilgrimage is too worldly, too materialistic, and too physical. Yet, this failed attempt at spirituality points our attention to the Parson, indicating the pilgrim whose tale will offer the opportunity to transcend the material world and to complete the true spiritual pilgrimage. The Man of Law does not—indeed cannot—provide the devotional tale he aspires to tell. But his desire for a more spiritual kind of narrative, though flawed and ultimately unsuccessful, sets us on the right path, the road that will lead not to Canterbury but to God's grace.

---

33 *The Parson's Prologue*, line 29 and *The Epilogue to the Man of Law's Tale*, line 1166.
34 *The Parson's Prologue*, lines 30–60.
35 *The Parson's Prologue*, line 72.

Conclusions

Unreliable narrator though the Man of Law might be, his tale nevertheless helps steer the pilgrims onto the path to spiritual redemption.[36] Through his retelling of a popular devotional tale, the Man of Law both responds to the debate about Fate and Free Will initiated by the Knight and, ultimately if not immediately, points towards the Parson, the one pilgrim who can bring the company closer to divine grace and to spiritual understanding. The Man of Law and his tale thus serve as bridges between the tales of the First Fragment, sophisticated narratives that pose important questions but that also lead the pilgrims to err from their true purpose, to the redemptive message of *The Parson's Tale*.

Building on the work of Chaucerian scholars who see *The Man of Law's Tale* as providing a new beginning to *The Canterbury Tales*, I propose that Chaucer here affirms his stance on important contemporary religious debates.[37] Through the Man of Law, Chaucer returns the pilgrims' attention to Thomas Becket and the pilgrimage. Having begun their journey towards Canterbury and Becket's shrine, the pilgrims are diverted from their original pious purpose by the tales of the First Fragment, stories that invite them to question the extent to which individuals can shape and control their lives. The Man of Law then redirects their attention towards Becket and the pilgrimage in two ways, first by invoking the Becket legend, thereby reminding his fellow pilgrims of the shrine towards which they are headed, and further by underscoring Custance's complete submission to God's will.

However, the Man of Law does not merely return the pilgrims' attention towards Becket and Canterbury; rather, Chaucer uses *The Man of Law's Tale* to point in the direction of the true aim of the pilgrimage, namely the Parson and his message about redemption. Through the Host's words to the Parson in the *Endlink*, the pilgrimage is imbued with a spiritual tone hitherto missing from the storytelling competition. Of course, the muted dispute between the Host and the Parson and the fact that the Parson does not give his sermon until much later show that the Man of Law does *not* succeed at bringing the rest of the company to the Parson's feet. Nevertheless, the *Endlink* at the very least positions *The Man of Law's Tale* and *The Parson's Tale* as bookends: if *The Parson's Tale* ends the collection by providing the pilgrims with a clear itinerary to God's grace, *The Man of Law's Tale* initiates the pilgrims' journey towards the Parson and his redemptive treatise. In the end, the most significant aspect of *The Man of Law's Tale* is that it creates a space to introduce the Parson and prepares the pilgrims for his tale.

In making this connection between *The Man of Law's Tale* and *The Parson's Tale*, Chaucer glosses on the role of popular devotional piety in the worshipper's journey towards God. Like the Becket legend, *The Man of Law's Tale* represents a kind of hagiography infused with romance elements and meant to appeal to lay audiences. That the *Endlink* does not succeed in convincing the Parson to preach his sermon suggests that popular devotional literature does not suffice to lead to true spiritual understanding.

---

[36] As argued by Michael Calabrese in *"The Man of Law's Tale* as a Keystone to *The Canterbury Tales,"* amongst others.

[37] Schibanoff, "Worlds Apart," 59–60; Harty, "The Tale and Its Teller," 361; and Shoaf, "'Unwemmed Custance,'" 298.

Yet, such works nevertheless constitute a first step towards God, an initiation on the way to a more complete understanding of the believer's relationship with and path to the divine.

Like his tale as a whole, the Man of Law's approach to conversion is flawed and needs revision. For the Man of Law, Christian virtue means allowing oneself, like Custance, to become God's tool. In *The Man of Law's Tale*, complete surrender to God's will is crucial. As for proselytizing, it remains the larger goal, the use to which God puts His faithful servants. Although the conversion of the heathen clearly plays a less important role in *The Man of Law's* Tale than it does in Nicholas Trivet's *Anglo-Norman Chronicles* and the *Confessio amantis* of John Gower, it nevertheless remains the objective to be pursued, however weakly and passively, by a virtuous Christian believer.

By contrast, the Parson reveals the belief in missionary work to be erroneous. It is not through proselytizing that the sinful soul may seek redemption. Rather, a true Christian must journey inwards to reach a state of contrition and find a way back to God. Where the Man of Law advocates for a traditional, missionary approach to virtue, one according to which the believer will earn God's grace through the surrender of the self in the object of bringing non-believers into the Christian fold, the Parson encourages individual self-introspection. The Other has no place in the path to the divine, the Parson suggests; what matters are the ties binding the soul to God.

Yet, the same impetus for self-introspection, contrition, and the desire to do penance and make amends for one's sins can be read into *The Man of Law's* Tale. If, as Schibanoff argues, "Kolve's Man of Law rallies the faithful by presenting them the narrative of Custance's spiritual journey to emulate in their own travel to Canterbury," Custance can also be seen as the personification of the human soul, buffeted by forces beyond her control from one shore to another.[38] Such an analysis of the tale may explain its relatively "happy" ending. Perhaps the Roman emperor stands for the divine and Custance must be sent away to do good deeds before she can regain entrance into her father's realm. What initially appears to result from the Man of Law's lack of deeper spiritual understanding may, in fact, reveal the need for a more allegorical reading of the tale. According to this interpretation of *The Man of Law's Tale*, the tale does not so much renounce—or even diminish—the power of conversion as redefine the term to describe an individualized, personal experience.

At line thirteen of *The General Prologue*, we are told that pilgrims long to "seken straunge strondes" (to seek the stranger strands), seeking out "ferne halwes" (far-off saints) but also Canterbury.[39] With these lines, Chaucer introduces us to the dichotomy between the foreign and the familiar while, in the same breath, stressing that these two polar opposites sometimes converge. The paradoxical duality of *The General Prologue*'s opening lines is echoed in *The Man of Law's Tale*, Chaucer once again using the word "straunge / strange" to indicate the difficulties inherent to identifying and distinguishing between the foreign and the familiar, us and them. On the day of Custance's departure for Syria, we are told that she cries because she must leave her home for a "strange

38 Schibanoff, "Worlds Apart," 60.
39 *The General Prologue*, lines 13, 14, and 16, respectively; Chaucer, *The Canterbury Tales*, 19.

nacioun" (stranger-nation).[40] A few hundred lines later, Donegild is said to deplore King Alla's wedding to Custance because the latter is too "strange a creature" (foreign creature).[41] Just as in *The General Prologue*, the word "strange" shifts sides with disturbing ease, deployed both to describe the heroine's fear of the Other and that felt by the pagan Other for her. In the end, where do "we" end and "they" start? And how can we speak of converting the Other in a world where difference and Otherness are constantly shifting, eluding us just as we seem on the verge of grasping them?

---

40 *The Man of Law's Tale*, lines 267–68; Chaucer, *The Canterbury Tales*, 147.
41 *The Man of Law's Tale*, line 700; Chaucer, *The Canterbury Tales*, 159.

CONCLUSION

In Chapter XXXVII of the first part of Miguel Cervantes's *Don Quixote*, the reader is introduced to Lela Zoreida, an Algerian noblewoman who has fled her homeland and seeks to be baptized.[1] A poignant exchange ensues Zoreida's introduction, one in which she insists that she be called "Maria" rather than "Zoreida." Her clothes mark her as a Moor and she possesses no Spanish; yet, she asks to be treated as a Christian rather than a Muslim. At first, this request seems likely to be granted: one of the other guests at the inn, Luscinda, comforts the agitated Zoreida with assurances that she will be called Maria.[2] Over the next several chapters, however, it become increasingly clear that, despite all of the sacrifices she has made to become a Christian, Zoreida remains a Moor to those around her. Zoreida's difference cannot be erased by her intent to convert or even, it is suggested, by baptism. Zoreida's name, her clothing, and her language root her firmly in her Algerian, Muslim past and make it seemingly impossible to adopt the faith and identity she claims has been hers since she was a young child. Although Zoreida has given up wealth, family, and home to receive baptism, her intentions matter very little to other Christians and how they perceive her.

 Don Quixote is an early modern, Spanish product, a work written after the expulsion of Jews and Muslims from Spain and one hardly revealing of late medieval English attitudes towards the Muslim Other. Yet, Geraldine Heng has compellingly argued that the roots of racialization emerge in the thirteenth and fourteenth centuries in England. I would add that several thirteenth- and fourteenth-century narratives reveal a heightened anxiety about difference, questioning the power of baptism and conversion while simultaneously emphasizing other markers of difference such as clothing and language. Josian of *Bevis of Hampton* and Thomas Becket's non-Christian mother of the Becket legend pave the way, I would argue, for the much later Lela Zoreida.

 Fourteenth-century English literary works document an increasing concern regarding conversion. *The King of Tars*, for example, reveals a deep-seated fear for the spiritual welfare of Christians thrust into pagan cultures and societies. Through the nameless princess of Tars, we witness a Christian believer who comes to act and pass as a Saracen, even going so far as to swear fealty to Saracen idols publicly. The same text also highlights the dangers inherent to religious miscegenation, this time by presenting the offspring of the Christian princess and her Saracen husband, the sultan of Damascus, as a lifeless lump of flesh. The poem thus exposes several anxieties associated with Christian exposure to other faiths and presents conversion as a double-edged sword.

 Bevis of Hampton, another fourteenth-century English poem, deepens and complicates the issues raised in *The King of Tars*. While fear that the Christian hero will be seduced into renouncing his faith remains a significant theme in *Bevis of Hampton*, particularly in the first half of the work, the longer poem also poses other, more complex questions. Through Josian, Bevis's Saracen lover and wife, the poem's composer(s) ques-

---

[1] Miguel de Cervantes, *Don Quixote*, trans. Edith Grossman (New York: Penguin, 2003), 325.
[2] Cervantes, *Don Quixote*, 327.

tions the mechanics of conversion: what makes it possible for one to become Christian? Is baptism enough? Or does that sacrament merely mark the initial step in this essential transformation? To what extent can we trust a new convert? Josian's lengthy journey from a Saracen princess into a fully-fledged Christian lady shows that baptism is no longer sufficient in determining a new convert's identity. Her murder of Earl Miles further illustrates an uncanny propensity for deception and treachery. Although Josian is presented as a victim of Miles's harassment, the passage nevertheless makes it clear that the Saracen princess is adept at deception and manipulation. Moreover, her Saracen companion, the giant Ascopard, is used to test the limits of conversion, suggesting that some are simply not eligible for admission into the Christian fold.

In contrast to *The King of Tars* and *Bevis of Hampton*, the Becket legend replaces the Anglo-Norman historical mother of St. Thomas Becket with a wholly fabricated heathen or Saracen—and in one text, Jewish—princess divinely guided to conceive the great English saint with Gilbert Becket. In the legend, Thomas's mother must be non-Christian to stress that his conception and birth was divinely ordained. Yet, here too, anxiety about conversion manifests itself after the princess's marriage and baptism—and the conception of Thomas Becket—through the need to add a concluding episode that shows Becket's mother struggling to assimilate into English society. She eventually succeeds, but the very need for the final scene in which Thomas's mother argues that her new husband can return to the Holy Land as long as he leaves her with the servant that knows her language highlights the narrative's lack of comfort with the princess's difference. On the one hand, the legend seeks out alterity, transforming a historically Christian character into a non-Christian one, and, on the other, it also needs to resolve and erase that pesky, troublesome Otherness once it has served its purpose.

These three texts utilize socio-cultural factors such as dress and language as markers of difference. In *The King of Tars*, the princess of Tars's false conversion, one that appears disturbingly close to a genuine one at the beginning of the work, is initiated by her donning the clothes typically worn by Saracen women. This act is followed shortly thereafter by her practicing the same customs as her husband, the Saracen Sultan of Damascus, and pretending to pray and worship at his idols' altars. *Bevis of Hampton* focuses slightly less on such socio-cultural factors; yet, Josian, Bevis's Armenian lover and wife, can only truly be accepted into the Christian fold once she has let go of her Saracen lore, knowledge, and customs and after severing her relationship with the Saracen giant Ascopard. Finally, linguistic difference looms large in the Becket legend, where Thomas's future mother is viewed as a beast and a strange creature precisely because of her inability to speak English when she first arrives in London. These three English works from the thirteenth and fourteenth centuries thus privilege socio-cultural markers of difference over religious ones, highlighting that assimilation into a new religious system is intertwined with learning to act, speak, and worship like other individuals within that system.

Where narratives such as *The King of Tars*, *Bevis of Hampton*, and the Becket legend present contradictory approaches to the conversion of the Muslim Other, The *Man of Law's Tale* simply rejects the missionary ideal personified in Custance. While *The King of Tars*, *Bevis of Hampton*, and the Becket legend all raise important doubts and questions about conversion, *The Man of Law's Tale* accentuates late medieval English anxieties about conversion and the Other and ultimately concludes that converting the heathen is not worth the trouble. As such, *The Man of Law's Tale* seems to represent the logical conclusion to which the other texts lead. If *The King of Tars*, *Bevis of Hampton*, and the Becket legend appear confused as to whether to celebrate or fear the conversion of the Other, *The Man of Law's Tale* proudly endorses its renunciation of missionary objectives.

This diminished interest in proselytizing and conversion is evident both in a reading of *The Man of Law's Tale* and in a more sophisticated analysis of the tale's function and place within the larger context of *The Canterbury Tales*. The Man of Law greatly reduces Custance's agency and, therefore, her missionary activity in comparison to Chaucer's primary source, Nicholas Trivet's *Anglo-Norman Chronicles*, as well as John Gower's *Confessio Amantis*. Moreover, the Man of Law changes the ending of the tale, rewarding Custance's successful missionary enterprise by allowing her to live with her father in Rome for an undetermined amount of time. The Man of Law, who claims he heard the story from merchants, presents Custance as disengaged and ultimately lacking in enthusiasm for her divine mission. Proselytizing is a task Custance must undertake before she can return to Rome, but she does not seem to enjoy or take any pleasure in bringing the various Others she encounters to God.

Despite the nearly unanimous understanding of the Man of Law as an unreliable narrator, his tale serves a crucial role in returning the pilgrims on the way to Canterbury to thoughts of pilgrimage and in pointing to the Parson in the *Endlink*. In doing so, Chaucer uses the tale to redefine the ideal of pilgrimage from one that involves physical travel to "straunge strondes" to one that must take place inside the believer's heart and soul. No longer merely a short voyage to the nearby shrine of Thomas Becket at Canterbury, the true pilgrimage necessitates an inward journey through penance and contrition to divine grace and redemption. At the end of *The Canterbury Tales*, the Parson tacitly argues that the conversion of the Other is not the ultimate spiritual goal and that there exist other, far more superior ways of remedying for one's sins than converting the heathen. In this renunciation of the conversion of non-Christians as an ideal to pursue to seek God's grace, the poet seems to echo and agree with the Man of Law.

The waning interest in conversion as a personal and collective spiritual goal outlined here and in the rest of this study does not take place all at once, and the growing indifference in proselytizing is not nearly as linear as I have made it seem above. Several later medieval works continue to place great emphasis on conversion and proselytizing despite the anxieties about conversion illustrated in works such as *The King of Tars*, *Bevis of Hampton*, the Becket legend, and *The Man of Law's Tale*. These texts that retain an interest in conversion often show no interest in the socio-cultural dynamics which I have argued come to complement and eventually displace religious difference as the most important factor in identifying an unknown Other.

To illustrate the lack of linearity in the slow, gradual process by which socio-cultural factors come to dominate over religious difference, I will simply return one last time to the two versions of the Constance narrative that lie closest to *The Man of Law's Tale*, those of Nicholas Trivet and John Gower. Although Trivet and Gower both fashion their heroine into a missionary figure and, therefore, emphasize the need to convert the hea-

94   CONCLUSION

then, the two authors deal with attendant socio-cultural factors in strikingly different ways. Although neither Trivet nor Gower focus much on Constance's dress, customs, and language, Trivet emphasizes from the beginning of his version that the princess is learned "en diverses langages" (in diverse languages).[3] Trivet then further highlights linguistic difference by having his characters speak various languages when appropriate. For example, when Hermengild speaks to the blind man immediately before restoring his sight, she addresses him not in French or Latin but in Middle English.[4] Even when introducing herself to her Roman relatives in the third part of the story, Constance performs an act of translation, naming herself Couste instead of Constance "(qar issint lapelerent lez Sessoneys) (for thus the Saxons called her)."[5] Dress likewise plays a role in Trivet's narrative, the narrator remarking upon Constance's "estraunge atir" (strange attire) upon her arrival on the shores of Elda's castle.[6]

By contrast, Gower shows little to no interest in Constance's attire and language. Rather than explain Constance's conversion of the heathen merchants as a result of her prodigious knowledge, education, and virtue, as is the case in Trivet's version, Gower speaks of Constance's "gode name" (good name) and her "feith" (faith) without alluding to the language in which Constance and the merchants conversed.[7] In Gower's version of the tale, the only act of translation that remains consists of Constance's change of name upon her initial return to Rome. Although Constance's adopted name is not described as the Saxon version of her given name when Constance first chooses it, it is glossed at the end of the tale when Alla alone recognizes the name and its real meaning.[8] Here, however, it is less linguistic difference than Alla's special position as the one individual capable of decoding Constance's verbal enigma that is privileged. The tales of Trivet and Gower themselves thus show the range of interest in various markers of difference—religious and not—in late medieval English literature.

Even much later literature sometimes favours religious identity at the expense of any other kind of marker of difference. In Thomas Malory's *Le Morte D'Arthur*, for example, the Saracen knight Palomides serves an important function as Sir Tristram's foil and rival throughout *The Book of Sir Tristram*. In this lengthy chapter, Palomides is repeatedly and emphatically differentiated from Tristram and other knights through his religion, one that, it is suggested, hinders him from reaching his full martial potential. Yet, at no point is Palomides described as wearing clothes that set him aside from his peers or as speaking an unfamiliar language. Not only does Palomides dress and speak like the other knights of the Round Table, but he also seems to be anchored just as firmly in the social fabric of Arthur's Britain.[9] Perhaps Palomides's lack of non-religious difference

---

3 Schlauch, "*The Man of Law's Tale*," 165; my translation.
4 Schlauch, "*The Man of Law's Tale*," 170.
5 Schlauch, "*The Man of Law's Tale*," 177; my translation.
6 Schlauch, "*The Man of Law's Tale*," 168; my translation.
7 Schlauch, "*The Man of Law's Tale*," 181, lines 596 and 598, respectively; my translation.
8 Schlauch, "*The Man of Law's Tale*," 201, lines 1405–6.
9 Palomides's mother resides close enough that he can pass by her castle and request food,

is the reason the Arthurian court absorbs him so completely after he finally converts at the end of *The Book of Sir Tristram*. In the final three books focusing on the Grail quest, Guinevere's affair with Launcelot, and the death of Arthur, Palomides is only mentioned in passing as one of the knights who supported Launcelot.[10] Having relinquished the faith that made him an outsider, Palomides has simply become another knight, indistinguishable from any other save by his loyalty to Launcelot. Malory's predilection for religious difference and his goal of proselytizing and conversion is further reinforced at the very end of the work, where the last of Arthur's knights to have survived the final battle against Modred die fighting against the infidel in the Holy Land on Good Friday.[11] In this respect, Malory's work lies closer to twelfth-century *chansons de geste* that conclude with the baptism of a principal pagan character than to fourteenth-century Middle English texts hesitant about the value of missionary work.

However, the ambivalence for proselytizing found in such works as *The King of Tars*, *Bevis of Hampton*, and the Becket legend and the fact that these narratives betray significant anxieties about conversion illustrates a marked shift in medieval English attitudes towards both the Other and the ideal of conversion. Although earlier poems such as the *Chanson de Roland* and the *Prise d'Orange* also hint at the fear that conversion might be used against the Christian heroes, these works are concerned with potentially insincere conversions. In the *Chanson de Roland*, for example, Marsile pretends that he and his followers will accept baptism to placate Charlemagne while having no intention to do so. At the same time, both the *Chanson de Roland* and the *Prise d'Orange* conclude on the climactic baptism of a Saracen princess. The baptisms of Bramimonde and Orable are perceived as genuine, life-altering events that transform two essential Saracen players into true, believing Christians. In both narratives, there appears no need to describe the convert's assimilation into Latin Christian society post-baptism. The only piece worth noting is that Bramimonde and Orable have chosen Christ. As such, they are casting aside their old, pagan identity and replacing it with a new, Christian one, and the two *chansons* end by renaming the Saracen women who have chosen baptism. By contrast, the identity of new converts to Christianity in the fourteenth-century English works discussed above remains shifting and malleable long *after* their baptism and supposed entry into Christian society. In these later works, the intent to convert, no matter how genuine and sincere, and even the act of baptism itself no longer guarantee assimilation and absorption into the Christian *communitas*.

There is no question that much work remains to be done on the changing perception of conversion in late medieval cultural artifacts. The present study seeks to highlight the changing perception of the Other as late medieval English authors begin to question their understanding of the world and the manner in which difference manifests itself. While further, more expansive study is necessary to trace the evolution and development

---

and he has inherited the hunt for the Questing Beast from the very Christian King Pellinore. For Palomides's visit to his mother, see Thomas Malory, *Complete Works*, ed. Eugène Vinaver, 2nd ed. (Oxford: Oxford University Press, 1971), 362.

10 Malory, *Complete Works*, 700.

11 Malory, *Complete Works*, 726.

of this shift, late medieval England, a territory both removed from intimate engagement with non-Christian communities—unlike Spain, for example—yet also known for its stark treatment of difference, provides an especially interesting case study with which to begin a larger study of this type.

Perhaps even more interesting in the case of late medieval England would be to juxtapose texts dealing with a variety of different Others to assess the specific rhetoric and imagery assigned to individual marginalized communities. The transformation of Thomas Becket's mother from an Anglo-Norman lady into a heathen princess into a Muslim noblewoman, and, finally, into a Jewish princess offers a fascinating entry point into a study of the treatment of Jews and Muslims in late medieval English texts. Why does Thomas's mother become Jewish in a fifteenth-century version of the legend? Would it have been possible for this character to be depicted as Jewish—rather than Saracen or broadly pagan—in earlier versions of the same narrative? And does the character change in other, more essential ways upon becoming Jewish? Examining the Becket legend with these questions in mind may give us important insights into how late medieval Europeans perceived alterity and differentiated amongst non-dominant, marginalized communities.

In "Invisible Translation, Language Difference and the Scandal of Becket's Mother," Robert Mills discusses two sets of visual representations of the Becket legend, the manuscript illuminations in the Queen Mary Psalter mentioned in the second chapter of this study and a "series of thirteen early sixteenth-century stained glass windows in York."[12] In describing the early modern stained glass windows, Robert Mills concludes that "as in the Queen Mary Psalter miniatures, the woman is differentiated sartorially, except that now her exotic costume remains even following conversion."[13] The goal of this study has been to apply this very same conclusion to late medieval English literature, noting that, just as with the visual representation of the Becket legend, 1) difference comes to be represented through the kind of socio-cultural marker emphasized in both the Queen Mary Psalter and in the York windows and 2) such markers become increasingly prominent in later texts, eventually achieving dominance over the sacrament of baptism.

The conclusions of this study suggest that the racialization of marginalized communities emerges not with the construction of the concept of race so much as with the deconstruction of the missionary ideal. Paired with diminished enthusiasm for missionary work is a changed attitude towards conversion, a new approach lending far less power to baptism. Where earlier narratives present baptism as a symbol of spiritual rebirth, thirteenth- and fourteenth-century texts increasingly question the ability of newly baptized converts to assimilate into English society post-conversion. The primary factor in identity formation seems to have shifted from religion to culture.

Finally, I wish to return one last time not to Becket's legendary mother but to Mandl. When I describe what happened to Mandl in Passau in 1477–78, I am told by other medievalists that what matters is not *what* was done to Mandl but *why*.[14] According to

---

12 Mills, "Invisible Translation," 143.
13 Mills, "Invisible Translation," 143.
14 Rubin, *Gentile Tales*, 87.

this view, the similarities I noted earlier do not matter; the only thing that truly signifies is whether or not Mandl's state-sanctioned murder can be determined to have resulted from an acknowledgement of his difference as based in his race or in his religion. If it can be proven that Mandl was forced to convert and beheaded because his Judaism had rendered him racially Other to his Christian neighbours, then his case belongs with that of Julius Jones and any number of nameless Black men condemned to the death penalty in our contemporary United States. If, however, we find ourselves unable to prove that Mandl's fate was determined based on racial intolerance, then there exists no meaningful connection between Mandl and Julius Jones.

Yet, I would argue that the similar fates of these men, separated by so much, yet also united by their common and undeserved suffering, does signify, and that the acts of hatred, injustice, and oppression perpetrated against them deserve our attention more than the label we assign to them. Both men faced persecution—and, more specifically, legal persecution—because they belonged to minority communities whom dominant groups were accustomed to harass and terrorize. Both men were sentenced to death; both men were silenced and rendered powerless. In the end, perhaps the fate of Mandl is the only thing that *does* really matter. If we can acknowledge that fact, then perhaps we can accept that racism is merely one of many ways of negatively treating the Other, of categorizing, separating, and creating hierarchies between the familiar and the unfamiliar, "us" and them.

So while Geraldine Heng advocates for the use of the word "race" in discussing the representation of Othered groups and individuals in medieval Europe because it carries a weight terms like "ethnicity" do not, I would argue that it is crucial to continue to question what Othering looked like in the Middle Ages and to determine the extent to which such processes align with modern racialization while nevertheless—and paradoxically—utilizing the term "race" to describe and discuss these practices. We must use the term "race" when addressing the Othering of minorities in medieval Europe because "race" is the word most clearly linked to Othering practices today. To do so is not to act anachronistically by projecting the practices of the present onto the past but to underscore the significance of past acts of oppression by using the terminology and language associated with persecution and intolerance today. To do so is to ensure that medieval acts of intolerance are not swept under the proverbial rug and relegated to obscure, antiquarian studies. To do so is to perform an act of translation that will enable us to explore human Othering practices in a more holistic manner. To do so it to prepare us for future Othering processes, ones that may or may not include racial elements but that will still lead to young people being tried and killed simply for being different.

BIBLIOGRAPHY

Ahmed, Sara. "Race as Sedimented History." *Postmedieval*, 6, no. 1 (2015): 94–97.
Akbari, Suzanne Conklin. *Idols in the East: European Representations of Islam and the Orient, 1100–1450*. Ithaca: Cornell University Press, 2009.
———. "Modeling Medieval World Literature." *Middle Eastern Literatures*, 20, no. 1 (2017): 2–17.
Bale, Anthony. "'A maner Latyn corrupt': Chaucer and the Absent Religions." In *Chaucer and Religion*, edited by Helen Phillips, 52–64. Woodbridge: Brewer, 2010.
———. *Feeling Persecuted: Christians, Jews, and Images of Violence in the Middle Ages*. London: Reaktion, 2011.
Barlow, Frank. *Thomas Becket*. Berkeley: University of California Press, 1986.
Barth, Fredrik, ed. *Ethnic Groups and Boundaries: The Social Organization of Culture Difference*. Long Grove: Waveland Press, 1998.
Bartlett, Robert. "Medieval and Modern Concepts of Race and Ethnicity." *Journal of Medieval and Early Modern Studies*, 31, no. 1 (Winter 2001): 39–56.
Bethencourt, Francisco. *Racisms from the Crusades to the Twentieth Century*. Princeton: Princeton University Press, 2014.
Birns, Nicholas. "'To Aleppo Gone': From the North Sea to Syria in Chaucer's *Man of Law's Tale* and Shakespeare's *Macbeth*." *Exemplaria*, 24, no. 4 (Winter 2012): 364–84.
Blurton, Heather and Jocelyn Wogan-Browne, eds. "Rethinking the *South English Legendaries*." In *Rethinking the South English Legendaries*, edited by Heather Blurton and Jocelyn Wogan-Browne, 3–19. Manchester: Manchester University Press, 2011.
Brault, Gerard J., trans. *La Chanson de Roland*. University Park: Pennsylvania University Press, 1984.
Brown, Carleton. "The Man of Law's Head-Link and the Prologue of *The Canterbury Tales*." *Studies in Philology*, 34, no. 1 (January 1937): 8–35.
Brown, Paul Alonzo. *The Development of the Legend of Thomas Becket*. Philadelphia: University of Pennsylvania Press, 1930.
Burge, Amy. *Representing Difference in the Medieval and Modern Orientalist Romance*. Basingstoke: Palgrave, 2016.
Burrow, J. "'A Maner Latyn Corrupt.'" *Medium Aevum*, 30, no. 1 (1961): 33–37.
Calabrese, Michael. "*The Man of Law's Tale* as a Keystone to *The Canterbury Tales*." In *Approaches to Teaching Chaucer's Canterbury Tales*, edited by Peter W. Travis and Frank Grady, 84–87. New York: Modern Language Association of America, 2014.
Calkin, Siobhain Bly. "The Anxieties of Encounter and Exchange: Saracens and Christian Heroism in *Sir Beves of Hamtoun*." *Florilegium* 21 (2004): 135–58.
———. "Marking Religion on the Body: Saracens, Categorization, and the *King of Tars*." *Journal of English and Germanic Philology*, 104, no. 2 (2005): 219–38.
———. "*The Man of Law's Tale* and Crusade." In *Medieval Latin and Middle English Literature: Essays in Honour of Jill Mann*, edited by Christopher Cannon and Maura Nolan, 1–24. Woodbridge: Brewer, 2011.
Cawsey, Kathy. "Disorienting Orientalism: Finding Saracens in Strange Places in Late Medieval English Manuscripts." *Exemplaria*, 21, no. 4 (Winter 2009): 380–97.
Caxton, William. *The Golden Legend or Lives of the Saints, as Englished by William Caxton*. London: Dent, 1928.
Cervantes. *Don Quixote*. Translated by Edith Grossman. New York: Penguin, 2003.

Chandler, John H., ed. *The King of Tars*. Kalamazoo: Medieval Institute Publications, 2015.
Chaucer, Geoffrey. *The Riverside Chaucer*. Edited by Larry D. Benson. 3rd ed. Boston: Houghton, 1987.
——. *The Canterbury Tales*. Translated by Nevill Coghill. 1971. Reprint, London: Penguin, 2003.
Chazan, Robert. *From Anti-Judaism to Anti-Semitism: Ancient and Medieval Christian Constructions of Jewish History*. Cambridge: Cambridge University Press, 2016.
Cohen, Jeffrey J. "On Saracen Enjoyment: Some Fantasies of Race in Late Medieval France and England." *Journal of Medieval and Early Modern Studies*, 31, no. 1 (2001): 111–44.
——. "Race." In *A Handbook of Middle English Studies*, edited by Marion Turner, 109–22. Chichester: Wiley, 2013.
Cooney, Helen. "Wonder and Immanent Justice in the *Man of Law's Tale*." *The Chaucer Review*, 33, no. 3 (1999): 264–87.
Cooper, Christine F. "'But algates therby was she understonde': Translating Custance in Chaucer's *Man of Law's Tale*." *The Yearbook of English Studies*, 36, no. 1 (2006): 27–38.
Davis, Kathleen. "Time Behind the Veil: The Media, the Middle Ages, and Orientalism Now." In *The Postcolonial Middle Ages*, edited by Jeffrey Jerome Cohen, 105–22. New York: St. Martin's, 2000.
D'Evelyn, Charlotte and Anna J. Mill, eds. *The South English Legendary*. Early English Text Society, o.s., 236. London: Oxford University Press, 1956–59.
De Weever, Jacqueline. *Sheba's Daughters: Whitening and Demonizing the Saracen Woman in Medieval French Epic*. New York: Routledge, 2015.
Dor, Juliette. "Chaucer's Viragos: A Postcolonial Engagement? A Case Study of the *Man of Law's Tale*, the *Monk's Tale*, and the *Knight's Tale*." In *Intersections of Gender, Religion and Ethnicity in the Middle Ages*, edited by Cordelia Beattie and Kirsten A. Fenton, 158–82. Basingstoke: Palgrave, 2011.
Eckert, Kenneth D. "Bad Animals and Faithful Beasts in *Bevis of Hampton*." *Neophilologus*, 97, no. 3 (2013): 581–89.
Ferrante, Joan, ed. and trans. *Guillaume d'Orange: Four Twelfth-Century Epics*. New York: Columbia University Press, 1974.
Frankis, John. "The Social Context of Vernacular Writing in Thirteenth-Century England: The Evidence of the Manuscripts." In *Rethinking the South English Legendaries*, edited by Heather Blurton and Jocelyn Wogan-Browne, 66–83. Manchester: Manchester University Press, 2011.
Fredrickson, George M. *Racism: A Short History*. Princeton: Princeton University Press, 2002.
Friedman, Jamie. "Making Whiteness Matter: *The King of Tars*." *postmedieval*, 6, no. 1 (2015): 52–63.
Furrow, Melissa. "Ascopard's Betrayal: A Narrative Problem." In *Sir Bevis of Hampton in Literary Tradition*, edited by Jennifer Fellows and Ivana Djordjević, 145–60. Cambridge: Brewer, 2008.
Goodman, Jennifer R. "Marriage and Conversion in Late Medieval Romance." In *Varieties of Religious Conversion*, edited by James Muldoon, 115–28. Gainesville: University of Florida Press, 1997.
Groebner, Valentin. "The Carnal Knowing of a Coloured Body: Sleeping with Arabs and Blacks in the European Imagination, 1300–1550." In *The Origins of Racism in the West*, edited by Miriam Eliav-Feldon, Benjamin Isaac, and Joseph Ziegler, 217–31. Cambridge: Cambridge University Press, 2009.
Harty, Kevin J. "The Tale and Its Teller: The Case of Chaucer's Man of Law." *The American Benedictine Review*, 34, no. 4 (1983): 361–71.

Heng, Geraldine. *Empire of Magic: Medieval Romance and the Politics of Cultural Fantasy*. New York: Columbia University Press, 2003.

——. "Jews, Saracens, 'Black Men,' Tartars: England in a World of Difference." In *A Companion to English Literature and Culture c. 1350–c. 1500*, edited by Peter Brown, 247–69. Oxford: Wiley, 2007.

——. "Reinventing Race, Colonizations, and Globalisms Across Deep Time: Lessons from *la Longue Durée*." *Publications of the Modern Language Association*, 130, no. 2 (2015): 358–66.

——. *The Invention of Race in the European Middle Ages*. Cambridge: Cambridge University Press, 2018.

Herzman, Ronald B., Graham Drake, and Eve Salisbury, eds. *Bevis of Hampton*. Kalamazoo: Medieval Institute Publications, 1999.

Hodges-Kluck, Katherine Lee. "The Matter of Jerusalem: The Holy Land in Angevin Court Culture and Identity, c. 1154–1216." PhD diss., University of Tennessee, 2015.

Horstmann, Carl, ed. "Thomas Beket, Epische Legende, von Laurentius Wade (1497)." *Englische Studien* III (1880): 409–69.

——, ed. *The Early South-English Legendary; or, Lives of Saints. I. Ms. Laud 108, in the Bodleian Library*. Early English Text Society, o.s., 87. London: Oxford University Press, 1887.

Hsy, Jonathan. "Translation Failure: The TARDIS, Cross-Temporal Language Contact, and Medieval Travel Narrative." In *The Language of Doctor Who: From Shakespeare to Alien Tongues*, edited by Jason Barr and Camille D. G. Mustachio, 109–23. Lanham: Rowman, 2014.

Hsy, Jonathan and Julie Orlemanski. "Race and Medieval Studies: A Partial Bibliography." *postmedieval*, 8, no. 4 (2017): 500–31.

Innocence Project. "Gov. Stitt Grants Julius Jones Clemency—8 Facts You Need to Know About his Case." https://innocenceproject.org/julius-jones-death-row-oklahoma-what-to-know/.

Johnson, William C., Jr. "Miracles in *The Man of Law's Tale*." *The Bulletin of the Rocky Mountain Modern Language Association*, 28, no. 2 (June 1974): 57–65.

Jones-Wagner, Valentina. "The Body of the Saracen Princess in *La Belle Helene de Constantinople*." *Bucknell Review*, 47, no. 2 (2004): 82–89.

Jordan, William C. "Why Race?" *Journal of Medieval and Early Modern Studies*, 31, no. 1 (2001): 165–73.

Kay, Sarah. *The Chansons de geste in the Age of Romance: Political Fictions*. Oxford: Clarendon, 1995.

Keita, Maghan. "Saracens and Black Knights." *Arthuriana*, 16, no. 4 (2006): 65–77.

Khanmohamadi, Shirin A. *In Light of Another's Word: European Ethnography in the Middle Ages*. Philadelphia: University of Pennsylvania Press, 2014.

Kim, Dorothy. "Reframing Race and Jewish/Christian Relations in the Middle Ages." *transversal*, 13, no. 1 (2015): 52–64.

Kinoshita, Sharon. "'Pagans are wrong and Christians are right': Alterity, Gender, and Nation in the *Chanson de Roland*." *Journal of Medieval and Early Modern Studies*, 31, no. 1 (Winter 2001): 79–111.

——. *Medieval Boundaries: Rethinking Difference in Old French Literature*. Philadelphia: University of Pennsylvania Press, 2006.

Kisor, Yvette. "Moments of Silence, Acts of Speech: Uncovering the Incest Motif in the *Man of Law's Tale*." *Chaucer Review*, 40, no. 2 (2005): 141–62.

Krummel, Miriamne. *Crafting Jewishness in Medieval England: Legally Absent, Virtually Present*. Basingstoke: Palgrave, 2011.

——, and Tison Pugh, eds. *Jews in Medieval England: Teaching Representations of the Other*. Basingstoke: Palgrave, 2017.

Lampert, Lisa. "Race, Periodicity, and the (Neo-) Middle Ages." *Modern Language Quarterly*, 65, no. 3 (2004): 391–421.
Lavezzo, Kathy. "Beyond Rome: Mapping Gender and Justice in *The Man of Law's Tale*." *Studies in the Age of Chaucer* 24 (2002): 149–80.
———. "Complex Identities: Selves and Others." In *The Oxford Handbook of Medieval English Literature*, edited by Elaine Treharne and Greg Walker, 434–57. Oxford: Oxford University Press, 2010.
———. *The Accommodated Jew: English Antisemitism from Bede to Milton*. Ithaca: Cornell University Press, 2016.
Legassie, Shayne Aaron. "Among Other Possible Things: The Cosmopolitanisms of Chaucer's 'Man of Law's Tale.'" In *Cosmopolitanism and the Middle Ages*, edited by John M. Ganim, 181–205. New York: Palgrave, 2013.
Lewis, Paula Gilbert. "The Contemporary Relevance of the Teaching of *La Chanson de Roland*: The Christian European Mind versus 'The Other.'" *College Language Association Journal*, 25, no. 3 (March 1982): 340–47.
Liszka, Thomas R. "*The South English Legendaries*." In *The North Sea World in the Middle Ages: Studies in the Cultural History of North-Western Europe*, edited by Thomas R. Liszka and Lorna E. M. Walker, 243–80. Dublin: Four Courts, 2001.
Lomperis, Linda. "Medieval Travel Writing and the Question of Race." *Journal of Medieval and Early Modern Studies*, 31, no. 1 (Winter 2001): 147–64.
Lomuto, Sierra. "The Mongol Princess of Tars: Global Relations and Racial Formation in *The King of Tars* (c. 1330)." *Exemplaria*, 31, no. 3 (2019): 172–88.
Lynch, Kathryn L. "Storytelling, Exchange, and Constancy: East and West in Chaucer's 'Man of Law's Tale.'" *The Chaucer Review*, 33, no. 4 (1999): 409–22.
Mallette, Karla. "The Hazards of Narration: Frame-Tale Technologies and the 'Oriental Tale.'" In *The Oxford Handbook of Chaucer*, edited by Suzanne Conklin Akbari and James Simpson, 184–96. Oxford: Oxford University Press, 2020.
Malory, Thomas. *Complete Works*. Edited by Eugène Vinaver. 2nd ed. Oxford: Oxford University Press, 1971.
Metlitzki, Dorothee. *The Matter of Araby in Medieval England*. New Haven: Yale University Press, 1977.
Middleton, Anne. "Chaucer's 'New Men' and the Good of Literature in the *Canterbury Tales*." In *Literature and Society*, edited by Edward W. Said, 15–56. Baltimore: Johns Hopkins University Press, 1980.
Mills, Robert. "Conversion, Translation and Becket's 'heathen' Mother." In *Rethinking the South English Legendaries*, edited by Heather Blurton and Jocelyn Wogan-Browne, 381–402. Manchester: Manchester University Press, 2011.
———. "The Early *South English Legendary* and Difference: Race, Place, Language, and Belief." In *The Texts and Contexts of Oxford, Bodleian Library, MS Laud Misc. 108: The Shaping of English Vernacular Narrative*, edited by Kimberly K. Bell and Julie Nelson Couch, 197–221. Leiden: Brill, 2011.
———. "Invisible Translation, Language Difference and the Scandal of Becket's Mother." In *Rethinking Medieval Translation: Ethics, Politics, Theory*, edited by Emma Campbell and Robert Mills, 125–46. Cambridge: Brewer, 2012.
De Miramon, Charles. "Noble Dogs, Noble Blood: The Invention of the Concept of Race in the Late Middle Ages." In *The Origins of Racism in the West*, edited by Miriam Eliav-Feldon, Benjamin Isaac, and Joseph Ziegler, 200–16. Cambridge: Cambridge University Press, 2009.

Morton, Nicholas. *Encountering Islam on the First Crusade*. Cambridge: Cambridge University Press, 2016.
Nadhiri, Aman Y. *Saracens and Franks in the 12th–15th Century European and Near Eastern Literature: Perceptions of Self and Other*. London: Routledge, 2017.
Netanyahu, Benzion. *The Origins of the Inquisition in Fifteenth Century Spain*. New York: Random House, 1995.
Nicholson, Peter. "Chaucer Borrows from Gower: The Sources of the *Man of Law's Tale*." In *Chaucer and Gower: Difference, Mutuality, Exchange*, edited by R. F. Yeager, 85–99. Victoria: University of Victoria, 1991.
Nirenberg, David. *Communities of Violence: Persecution of Minorities in the Middle Ages*. Philadelphia: University of Pennsylvania Press, 1996.
Rajabzadeh, Shokoofeh. "The Depoliticized Saracen and Muslim Erasure." *Literature Compass* 16 (2019): 1–8.
———. "Alisaundre Becket: Thomas's Resilient, Muslim, Arab Mother in *The South English Legendary*." *postmedieval*, 10, no. 3 (2019): 293–303.
Ramey, Lynn Tarte. *Christian, Saracen and Genre in Medieval French Literature*. New York: Routledge, 2001.
———. "Role Models? Saracen Women in Medieval French Epic. *Romance Notes*, 41, no. 2 (December 2001): 131–41.
———. *Black Legacies: Race and the European Middle Ages*. Gainesville: University Press of Florida, 2014.
Reames, Sherry. "*The South English Legendary* and Its Major Latin Models." In *Rethinking The South English Legendaries*, edited by Heather Blurton and Jocelyn Wogan-Browne, 84–105. Manchester: Manchester University Press, 2011.
Robertson, Elizabeth. "The "Elvyssh" Power of Constance: Christian Feminism in Geoffrey Chaucer's *Man of Law's Tale*." *Studies in the Age of Chaucer* 23 (2001): 143–80.
Rubin, Miri. *Gentile Tales: The Narrative Assault on Late Medieval Jews*. New Haven: Yale University Press, 1999.
Schibanoff, Susan. "Worlds Apart: Orientalism, Antifeminism, and Heresy in Chaucer's *Man of Law's Tale*." *Exemplaria*, 8, no. 1 (1996): 59–96.
Schlauch, Margaret. "*The Man of Law's Tale*." In *Sources and Analogues of Chaucer's Canterbury Tales*, edited by W. F. Bryan and Germaine Dempster, 155–206. Chicago: University of Chicago Press, 1941.
Shoaf, R. A. "'Unwemmed Custance': Circulation, Property, and Incest in *The Man of Law's Tale*." *Exemplaria*, 2, no. 1 (March 1990): 287–302.
Spearing, A. C. "Narrative Voice: The Case of Chaucer's *Man of Law's Tale*." *New Literary History*, 32, no. 3 (Summer 2001): 715–46.
Staunton, Michael. *The Lives of Thomas Becket*. Manchester: Manchester University Press, 2001.
Sturges, Robert S. "Race, Sex, Slavery: Reading Fanon with *Aucassin et Nicolette*." *postmedieval*, 6, no. 1 (2015): 12–22.
Sussman, Robert Wald. *The Myth of Race: The Troubling Persistence of an Unscientific Idea*. Cambridge, MA: Harvard University Press, 2014.
Swanson, R. N. *Religion and Devotion in Europe, c. 1215–c. 1515*. Cambridge: Cambridge University Press, 1995.
Thomas, James M. "The Racial Formation of Medieval Jews: A Challenge to the Field." *Ethnic and Racial Studies*, 30, no. 10 (2010): 1737–55.
Tomasch, Sylvia. "Bibliography: Medieval Antisemitism." *Medieval Feminist Forum: A Journal of Gender and Sexuality*, 16, no. 1 (1993): 38–43.

Tyler, Carole-Anne. "Passing: Narcissism, Identity, and Difference." *differences: A Journal of Feminist Cultural Studies*, 6, no. 2–3 (Summer–Fall 1994): 212–48.

Warner, Lawrence. "Adventurous Custance: St. Thomas of Acre and Chaucer's *Man of Law's Tale*." In *Place, Space, and Landscape in Medieval Narrative*, edited by Laura L. Howes, 43–59. Knoxville: University of Tennessee Press, 2007.

Weinstein, Donald and Rudolph M. Bell. *Saints and Society: Christendom, 1000–1700*. Chicago: University of Chicago Press, 1982.

Whitaker, Cord J. *Black Metaphors: How Modern Racism Emerged from Medieval Race-Thinking*. Philadelphia: University of Pennsylvania Press, 2019.

Williams Boyarin, Adrienne. "Inscribed Bodies: The Virgin Mary, Jewish Women, and Medieval Feminine Legal Authority." In *Law and Sovereignty in the Middle Ages and Renaissance*, edited by Robert S. Sturges, 229–51. Turnhout: Brepols, 2011.

Wood, Chauncey. "Chaucer's Man of Law as Interpreter." *Traditio* 23 (1967): 149–90.

Wood, Marjorie Elizabeth. "The Sultaness, Donegild, and Fourteenth-Century Female Merchants: Intersecting Discourses of Gender, Economy, and Orientalism in Chaucer's *Man of Law's Tale*." *Comitatus: A Journal of Medieval and Renaissance Studies* 37 (2006): 65–85.

Yeager, Suzanne M. "Fictions of Espionage: Performing Pilgrim and Crusader Identities in the Age of Chaucer.'" In *The Oxford Handbook of Chaucer*, edited by Suzanne Conklin Akbari and James Simpson, 197–215. Oxford: Oxford University Press, 2020.

Young, Helen. *Constructing "England" in the Fourteenth Century: A Postcolonial Interpretation of Middle English Romance*. Lewiston: Edwin Mellen, 2010.

INDEX

Acre, 56, 61
Alla, 8, 62, 63, 64, 65, 66, 67, 69, 70, 71, 72, 73, 74, 75, 90, 94
Aragon, 18
Armenia, 25, 26, 28, 29, 31, 32
  Armenian, 9, 11, 92
Ascopard, 29, 30, 31, 32, 33, 34, 92
baptism, 5, 6, 8, 9, 10, 12, 13, 14, 16, 19, 23, 29, 30, 31, 32, 33, 34, 38, 43, 45, 47, 51, 52, 58, 59, 60, 61, 68, 69, 70, 77, 91, 92, 95, 96
  baptismal 44, 70
Becket. *See* Gilbert Becket
Bevis, 25, 26, 27, 28, 29, 30, 31, 32, 33, 91, 92
Bevis of Hampton 4, 8, 9, 10, 11, 13, 14, 19, 25, 33, 34, 57, 60, 61, 77, 91, 92, 93, 95
Bramimonde 15, 16, 20, 23, 51, 57, 68, 95
Canterbury, 7, 35, 36, 42, 49, 50, 53, 56, 77, 79, 84, 85, 87, 88, 89, 93
Canterbury Tales 7, 8, 10, 69, 77, 82, 83, 84, 88, 93. *See also* General Prologue, Host, Parson
Cervantes, Miguel de, 91
Chanson de Roland, 13, 14, 15, 16, 17, 18, 23, 34, 51, 57, 60, 68, 95
Constance, 9, 19, 61, 63, 64, 72, 73, 74, 75, 81, 83. 84, 93, 94
crusade, 3, 51, 56, 57, 82
Custance, 7, 8, 9, 62, 63, 64, 65, 66, 67, 68, 69, 70, 71, 72, 73, 74, 75, 76, 82, 87, 88, 89, 90, 92, 93
Charlemagne, 15, 16, 18, 95
Donegild, 65, 69, 70, 71, 75, 90
Endlink, 10, 83, 84, 86, 87, 88, 93
Ermin, 25, 26, 27, 29
General Prologue 77, 79, 81, 82, 89, 90
Gilbert, 18, 19, 25
Gilbert Becket, 7, 8, 35, 38, 39, 40, 41, 42, 43, 44, 45, 46, 47, 48, 49, 50, 51, 52, 57, 58, 59, 60, 62, 64, 65, 67, 92
Gower. *See* John Gower
Guielin, 18

Guillaume, 17, 18, 19
Guy, 32
heathens, 8, 10, 21, 25, 32, 38, 43, 47, 48, 60, 62, 63, 64, 65, 67, 70, 89, 92, 93, 94, 96
  heathendom 46
Host, The, 79, 83, 84, 85, 86, 87, 88
John Gower, 61, 62, 64, 72, 73, 74, 75, 89, 93, 94
Josian, 9, 29, 30, 31, 32, 33, 34, 58, 60, 91, 92
Julius Jones, 1, 97
The King of Tars, 5 8, 9, 10, 13, 19, 20, 23, 24, 25, 31, 34, 51, 57, 60, 70, 73, 77, 91, 92, 93, 95
Later Quadrilogus 9, 35, 38, 39, 40, 42, 43, 46, 49, 52. *See also Quadrilogus* I
Legenda Aurea, 35, 41
  Middle English translation, 35, 48, 49, 51, 52, 56
London, 9, 32, 35, 36, 38, 41, 43, 44, 45, 48, 49, 50, 51, 52, 56, 57, 58, 62, 65, 75, 92
lump, 12, 22, 23, 91
  lump-child 22
Malory, Sir Thomas, 94, 95
Mandl, 1, 5, 96, 97
Marsile, 15, 16, 95
Maurice, 63, 66, 67, 70, 71, 73, 74, 75
Miles:
  Earl Miles, 31, 92
  son of Bevis and Josian, 32
missionaries, 9, 10, 68, 72, 73, 75, 76, 82, 89, 92, 93, 95, 96
Muslims, 3, 5, 6, 7, 8, 9, 10, 11, 12, 24, 31, 40, 48, 62, 68, 70, 77, 91, 92, 96
Nicholas Trivet, 9, 61, 62, 63, 64, 72, 73, 74, 75, 89, 93, 94
Northumberland, 8, 73
Orable, 17, 18, 19, 20, 51, 95
Orange, 18
pagans, 7, 8, 10, 38, 40, 47, 53, 66, 70, 90, 91, 95, 96
Palomides, 94, 95

Passau, 1, 96
Parson, The, 10, 83, 84, 85, 86, 87, 88, 89, 93
  Parson's Prologue, 87
  Parson's Tale, 83, 84, 85, 88
pilgrimage, 35, 38, 39, 40, 44, 45, 52, 58, 59, 60, 69, 84, 85, 86, 87, 88, 93
Princess of Tars, 20, 21, 22, 23, 25, 34, 73, 91
Prise d'Orange 9, 13, 17, 18, 24, 25, 34, 51, 58, 60, 95
Quadrilogus I, 35, 38
Queen Mary Psalter, 51, 52, 53, 96
Roland, 14, 16

Rome, 8, 66, 67, 73, 75, 76, 93, 94
Saracen princess, motif, 20, 40, 57, 61, 62, 66, 67
South English Legendary, 9, 35, 41, 42, 44, 46, 48, 49, 52, 53, 56
Spain, 2, 15, 16, 19, 91, 96
Sultan of Damascus, 8, 20, 23, 60, 70, 73, 91, 92
Sultan of Syria, 8, 61, 71, 73, 75
Tars. *See* Princess of Tars
Terri, 27, 28
Thomas of Acre, saint, 49, 50, 56, 61, 62, 64
Trivet. *See* Nicholas
Zoreida, 91

Printed in the United States
by Baker & Taylor Publisher Services